Daddy Day Care

A book for new dads and curious mums

Jonathan Tindale

For Squeaky and Padawan

Contents

Introduction

For the past six months, I lived in a strange and mysterious world. And no, I don't mean Papua New Guinea or the International Space Station. Strangely, you don't need to travel very far at all to find this place because it's right under your very nose - at home.

I'm a dad and instead of going to the office every day, I hung up my travelcard and embarked on a six-month rollercoaster ride of parenting. I suppose it was quite similar to a loop-the-loop. There was frequent screaming (hers), panic and terror (mine), a great deal of throwing up (hers again) and someone always shits their pants (no, that wasn't me).

There are a lot of terrific books out there, written by mums and for mums. This one is for the dads, soon-to-be dads and curious mums who are wondering what kind of disaster would occur if their other half stepped into their shoes.

Don't worry. This is not one of those parenting books where I jump up and down on my soap box telling you what to do. There's plenty of those already. God knows, we don't need another one. What this book is, is a pretty honest account of a dad finding his way through the swirling snot and poo soaked chaos of full-time childcare. I like to think a few of you might get to the end and think "well, if this idiot can look after his baby daughter everyday for six months, then maybe I (or my husband/partner) can do it too."

So, what is it like for a stay at home dad? Did you ever see those movies where the parent and kid swap places? The child discovers what it's really like to be a grown up and go to work, and the adult rediscovers what a merciless place school is? Daddy day care is a bit like that. It's a woman's world out there. This might be the twenty-first century, but parenting still feels like its mostly stuck in 1953. You're as likely to stumble across a leatherback sea turtle as you are to find a dad who looks after his baby whilst mum goes to work.

So, how is parenting different as a dad? Well, it's pretty similar to what a mum goes through, but with some extra tricky stuff. Where does a chap look when he's surrounded by exposed female nipples? What should a dad wear and why? How do you manage being the only bloke at playgroup? Can you get some DIY done? Who is Gina Ford and what is a bobbin and why do you need to wind the bobbin up? Can you spend the day in your pants watching DVDs? Why won't she nap? Why? Why? Please God, why wont she stop crying? What do you give her to eat? Why won't she poo? Why won't she stop pooing? And when all else fails, what would Darth Vader do?

The answers to all these questions and more may be found in the following pages. Uh, well maybe. To be honest, I'm not promising anything. I just drank a small bucket of coffee, my daughter is crying AGAIN and everything is going a bit fuzzy.

Note
In a spurious attempt at maintaining my family's privacy, I'll be referring to my daughter simply as Squeaky, due to her remarkable and frankly, relentless range of high-pitched squawks, screams and squeaks. I have a son too, who turned four during this time. He'll be making the occasional appearance. I'll be calling him my padawan. If you're unfamiliar with the intricacies of Star Wars, a padawan is like an apprentice, but with less plumbing and more lightsaber skills.

Gosh – it really is hard work isn't it?

I'll admit, I may have slightly underestimated the monumental task of looking after a baby full-time. When asked by family, what was I planning to do, I replied "I'm going to learn to play the guitar!" In fairness, I'd reasoned that since I was going to be singing nursery rhymes all day long, I might as well learn to play an instrument to accompany humpty dumpty and the owl and the pussycat.

I know, I should have known better, but it wasn't like I was a complete novice. After all, this was second time around for us. Our son was two years old when we discovered Amy was pregnant. I had been taking care of my Padawan every

Tuesday, since Amy's maternity leave had finished and I hadn't broken him yet. I'd also done my fair share of baby care. I could change a nappy. I figured I could probably make up a bottle of warm milk whilst blindfolded (hmm, but on second thoughts I'd not recommend it, considering the likelihood of a finger bath with boiling water).

And there was plenty of time to prepare. Oh, what an idiot, I was. Nine months of pregnancy went by in the blink of an eye. Then our lives entered a haze of sleepless nights and bumping into things. Before we both knew it, Amy was due to return to work. Endless months of potential preparation became reduced to a single yellow 'Post-it' note on the fridge, that simply read "8am brekkie. 10am nap. 12pm lunch. 2pm nap. 5pm? dinner. 7pm bed".

The truth is most of the preparation is psychological. The main difference between taking care of your little one whilst your wife or partner has a nap is that you are only temporarily in charge. Like a Vice President or Deputy Prime Minister you have only been given temporary custody, under the strict understanding you can't reverse any policies, or invade anywhere you don't like the look of, or do anything at all really. It's quite a different situation when your other half leaves for work at 6am and you know she won't be back for twelve hours. Then you are in charge. Why is my baby crying? Is she hungry? Is she thirsty? Is she tired? Is she dirty? Does she just want some attention? It's on you now. Sure, you can make a phone call and ask for advice, but all the decisions and responsibilities are now yours.

One of the first things that became quickly apparent was that instead of an interminably long stretch of time before my wife returned home, the hours flashed by in a rapid and repeated sequence of holding Squeaky, making up her milk bottles and – when she refused to nap – putting her in the pushchair and walking until she stopped crying (yes, I did get dressed first, I am house trained you know).

It was hard going at times and it would be some weeks before I'd say I was tuned into her needs and learned to recognise 'I'm sleepy and grouchy' from 'I'm hungry and grouchy'. But there is little preparation for that, you just have to learn on the job.

We got through the day with the simple ambition of surviving until Amy returned. I may even have succeeded in folding the laundry but I'm pretty sure I didn't manage anything as ambitious as preparing dinner. I quickly learned if you're hoping to achieve anything beyond surviving the whirlwind of life as a stay at home parent you need to have a plan.

A day in
the life

Having a plan is important. My daily routine started off as a post-it note on the fridge door. Within a couple of weeks it had grown into an inch thick battle plan indelibly burned into my brain.

I always tried to be a bit flexible with the plan. I don't subscribe to the synchronized watches school of mechanical parenting, or at least I didn't think I did. Sometimes, I'd be a bit spontaneous and offer my daughter a bottle at 10:30am, rather than 10am, if for instance she'd had a longer morning nap. If I strayed too far from her daily schedule Squeaky would promptly remind me with an ear splitting scream, which could be loosely translated as "GOD DAMN IT, MAN! WHERE'S MY MILK?! IF THIS WAS DOWNTON ABBEY, YOU'D BE SACKED AND BACK DOWN THE MINE BY NOW!"

I never for a moment thought that looking after my baby daughter for the day would be easy. I really didn't, but I was taken aback at how much work it would be and how little time I would have.

Did you ever return home from a hard day at work to discover a pile of dirty laundry on the floor, your other half exhausted, prostrate on the sofa and a bowl of coco pops for tea? I must clarify that my wife, Amy, against insurmountable odds always managed to put a home cooked meal on the table for us. God knows how, but she did. I'd be grateful and ask how her day was and she would perhaps say she'd met with some friends for a coffee or put the washing machine on. It never sounded like much, but I always suspected there was more to her day than she'd say. I've now come to realize that it wasn't that she was modest as such, it's just she was too exhausted to even begin to recall the never ending pile of small tasks that occupied her day. So, if you ever wondered what the hell's so time consuming about caring for a little person, here is a typical day:

Morning

5am	Alarm goes off. Amy gets up very quietly (NO! DON'T FLUSH THE TOILET) to catch the train to Birmingham.
5.30am	Quick shower whilst kids are still asleep (and I'm not being screamed at – yay!)
5.40am	Squeaky wakes up.
6.30am	Prepare milk, sterilise bottle, boil water, mix formula, cool bottle
6.50am	Sit down, give Squeaky her bottle. Remote control for TV is three inches out of reach so I stare out the window and imagine there's 'breaking news' where you can buy sleep by the hour at all good convenience shops
7.05am	Padawan wakes up 'Daddy!!!' Carry Squeaky upstairs in mid-milk glug and bring Padawan downstairs

7.30am	Pack both kids in the car to take Padawan to nursery
7.45am	Prepare Squeaky's breakfast (burn toast, start again, butter toast, cut toast, or spoon feed porridge)
8am	Spend best part of an hour offering toast/poking porridge at Squeaky who insists on picking it up and dropping it on the floor
9am	Wipe Squeaky down. Wipe high chair down. Consider throwing high chair into garden and hosing it down. Wash up. Sweep floor. Wipe porridge off the ceiling with profound wonder at how it got up there
9.30am	Squeaky is squeaking. Nap time. Put her down to sleep. Load washing machine.
9.40am	Still screaming. Hold Squeaky. She falls asleep. Put her down. She wakes up, screaming
10am	Put her in pushchair, fly out of front door
10.05	She's asleep. Enjoy a brief flood of happiness and the satisfaction of mission accomplished
10.10	Race home quickly to make the most of the peace and quiet
10.15am	Put kettle on
10.20am	Go to the toilet. Read page 56 of a book I have been reading for the last three months
10.25am	Make tea. Look in fridge
10.30am	Squeaky wakes up - squeaking
10.45am	Remember I made a cup of tea, that has since gone cold. Down tea in one glug.

10.50am   Arrange toys on floor and start to think about
          lunch, think about sorting post, think about
          having a shower. It's all too much

11am   Change nappy. Get Squeaky dressed

11.20   Clean my teeth whilst holding baby with one
          arm, accidentally insert toothbrush up left nostril,
          sneeze, baby cries

11.30   Prepare lunch for Squeaky (about 20 minutes)

11.50   Prepare lunch for self (about 2 minutes) Fold
          slice of bread around lump of cheese and
          consider myself lucky

Afternoon

12.00   Spend the next hour watching Squeaky
          redistribute her lunch across an area the size of
          the New Forest

1.00pm   Wipe, sweep, mop detritus from pushchair,
          floor, surrounding furniture and from her face,
          hair, chin, ear, nose and feet

1.30pm   Throw clothes on washing line. Switch TV on

1.35pm   Spend 10 minutes watching someone auction
          a small, slightly broken, antique for £40 whilst
          singing 'Row, row, row your boat' with hand
          movements

1.40pm   Squeaky yawns, poops and cries (again)

1.45pm   Change nappy (nasty)

1.50pm   Put Squeaky in pushchair, grab change bag and
          head out

2.10pm   Baby asleep

2.15pm   Walk past pub amidst fond memories of a carefree pint or three

2.30pm   Stumble into generic Pret-a-Bucks coffee shop. Order latte and a slice of something sweet and sticky (because, by the gods, I deserve it) and very gently park pushchair. Sit down. Relax...

2.40pm   Coffee arrives, a little too hot to drink so I check pushchair, confident she is asleep. Squeaky stares back at me - wide awake, demanding I pick her up

2.50pm   Drink coffee whilst standing up and holding Squeaky in one arm. Familiar but unwanted warm sensation in palm of hand. Shove cake in mouth in two swift gulps

2.55pm   Burp my way to the toilets to discover there are no change facilities, despite the shop being filled with mums and infants

3.00pm   March home as Squeaky howls at me and mentally invent the 'Poop app' that will direct me to the nearest changing facilities

3.10pm   Get home. Change baby. She falls asleep again.

3.15pm   Sit down before I fall down. Read page 57 of book. Confused. Reread page 56. Abandon book. Wonder if it's acceptable to give family Coco Pops for dinner.

3.20pm   Prepare milk, sterilise bottle, boil water, mix formula, leave bottle to cool

3.25pm   Watch half an episode of Twin Peaks before nodding off for three minutes

3.20pm   Strange dream of being trapped in a red room
           with Dale Cooper, a small backwards talking
           man and a screaming baby. Wake up in cold
           panic

3.30pm   Sit down, give Squeaky her bottle.

4.00pm   Play time. Nursery rhymes mostly, some boisterous
           bouncing and maybe a dance or two. Squeaky has
           discovered her toes. I almost cry with happiness

5.00pm   Prepare meal, taking great care not to chop
           fingers off thus inventing the 'finger salad' due
           to total exhaustion

5.40pm   Collect Padawan from nursery. Squeaky squeaks
           whilst being put in car, squeaks en-route and on
           way home

Evening

6.00pm   Amy arrives home, asks how my day was and I
          realize I have absolutely no idea where the day
          went

6.30pm   Watch my dinner go cold as I feed Squeaky

7.00pm   Run bath for both kids. Squeaky loves the
          water. Lift her from bath. Squeaky cries.
          Dry and dress her as she screams in my ear.
          Padawan complains that Squeaky is giving him
          a headache. We try not to laugh hysterically

8.00pm   Prepare milk, sterilise bottle, boil water, mix
          formula, cool bottle

8.30pm   Put sleeping baby down once, twice, three times,
          lose count, before she finally goes down

9.00pm   Pour two glasses of wine. We think about
          watching a DVD, mention watching a film,
          attempt to have a conversation that doesn't
          mention boo-boos, poop, bum nuggets or
          exploding weetabix

10pm   We go to bed. Pooped.

10.05pm   Pass out

Night-time

1.00am	Squeaky squeaks herself awake, wakes us up, before falling asleep again
2am	Squeaky wakes up crying. Pick Squeaky up. Squeaky throws up. Change. Dump dirty clothes on bathroom floor.
2.15am	Pick up Squeaky, put down Squeaky x 6 (that is, six times, not six babies, good grief, that's a sobering thought)
2.40am	Still holding Squeaky, put her down for the seventh time and she doesn't wake up, but now I'm wide awake
2.45am	Stare at the swirls and stipples in the ceiling. I can feel my eyes pop out on stalks like a Looney Tunes cartoon
3.20am	Still staring at ceiling. Develop a deep and abiding dislike of artex
3.30am	Eventually fall back to sleep
3.55am	Squeaky screams. Pick her up, hold Squeaky
4.15am	Still holding baby, achieve the feat of briefly falling asleep whilst standing up, put baby down, she's asleep
4.30am	Fall asleep, exhausted
5am	Alarm goes off (repeat, as before)

Local playgroups

The godfather of soul and world's funkiest man, James Brown was pretty insistent when he sang "It is a man's world" or rather "IT IS A MAN'S WORLD". In most respects he would be right. Men tend to be Presidents, Prime Ministers (and despots), they run international corporations and take the lions share of sports prizes and cash. Of course, women also do these things but are much fewer in number and tend to be exceptions to the rule. It is a man's world, no?

Well, not from this side of the pushchair it's not. One of the first things I noticed as a stay at home dad was that after 9am, when everyone else had gone out to work, my local village changed. As if out of nowhere, boards for 'Play Tots' and 'Little Stars' appeared. Every available village hall, church hall, brownie hut and library was given over to nursery facilities. Legions of women with pushchairs would appear, marching towards these destinations, or failing that, a coffee shop.

One day, I decided to take the plunge and follow them into one such nursery.

The playgroup was remarkably civilised. There were cups of tea and biscuits, a nice sing-song and plenty of toys to distract the little ones. I'll admit I was somewhat disturbed by two infants operating on a doll with a plastic hammer - their mothers oblivious to their loved ones playing out a scene from a horror movie.

As a dad, I had fully expected myself to be in the minority here. Still, I was surprised to discover that I would typically be the only chap amongst twenty or thirty mums. It was like the 'smurfete principle' (a TV show with a cast of men and precisely one token female, like The Smurfs) but in reverse.

I wondered how the mums would react to me - this cuckoo in their nest, or rather a cock in the coop. I expected the worst. An acquaintance, Bob, had told me how he'd brought up his baby twins full-time. "My wife wasn't happy being home with the twins," he explained. "She went back to work and I stayed home with them from about three months. I loved it and now they're older, I have a much stronger relationship with the kids than if I'd been at the office. But one time, I took them to a local nursery. A mum came up to tell me that I couldn't bring the kids in because I was a man and that she'd have to discuss the matter with the other mums. Apparently they did decide to let us join them the following week, but I never went back."

I'm happy to say this was never my experience. Quite the contrary, in fact I was taken aback at how helpful mums were. One time, I found myself suddenly and unexpectedly with a hand full of baby snot and without my wet wipes. I was just about to discreetly smear my hands over my trousers when, as if out of nowhere, a mum appeared with a friendly smile and offered me a wet wipe. And this really wasn't unusual.

There appears to be some tacit understanding that you help out a fellow mum in need, and by extension help out a dad too. Rather than being an unpleasant intruder in a woman's world, I was accepted pretty quickly into whichever group of mums I found myself with. If anything, as a dad with a baby you're something of a novelty and I found mums to be very positive about the role reversal. If I had a fiver for every time a mum had said "I wish my husband/partner/ boyfriend was more hands on" I would have enough money to buy a modest, but scenic, Greek island.

Bluffing your way with mum chat

L et's assume you have abandoned your status as local hermit, you found your local playgroup and the mums have welcomed you.

You are now going to find yourself in what can only be described as woman-only chats. You know, that awkward moment when the conversation moves to lactating nipples, gruesome caesareans and graphic labour pains. Mums often bond over such shared experiences. It reminds me of old war movies where unlikely friendships are struck when both characters discover they each fought alongside one another in the Battle of Iwo Jima.

These conversations can be very intimidating for mums as well as dads, as mums attempt to impress one another with their feats of endurance and survival. "Stitches up to your belly button? Lost two pints of blood? I wish I had it so easy, my epidural didn't work and I saw the whole show when my doctor almost sawed me in half, like I was bloody Debbie McGee!"

What do you say in these situations? Well, it's nod quietly time because my friend, you're deep, deep, deep out of your depth here. Trust me, mentioning the time you broke your arm whilst walking home drunk from the pub will do you no favours here.

You may find yourself being offered advice from well-meaning mums. As a dad, some mothers may feel they want to help you (or interfere) and you may, or may not be grateful for these pearls of wisdom. "Oh dear, is she tired? Does she need to sleep?" isn't especially useful when your little loved one is melting down like a Ukrainian nuclear reactor. If you note the odd judgemental frown, try and ignore it. Don't forget, everyone in the room is almost hallucinating from sleep deprivation. If you do find yourself cornered by some awful busy-body, who insists you need to give your child more vegetables/more hugs/let them cry at night/don't let them cry at night, then this is the perfect response. Just say "I'm following our paediatrician's advice, but thanks anyway." That will shut them up.

A lot of mums will be comparing notes, especially the first time parents. Everyone is desperate for confirmation that they're not horribly neglecting their beloved baby by giving him the occasional biscuit. Every playgroup will have at least one self-righteous mum who claims their child is being weaned on brussel sprouts and brown rice.

There is also a tendency for mums to be quite competitive about their offspring. I suppose we all are, to a degree. We all want to know that our baby is bright, beautiful and not behind in any respect. Almost without exception, the opening for a conversation will always be "How old is your daughter?" Nobody starts a chat with "So, what's your baby's name?" or "I'm Jennifer, nice to meet you" or that old British classic "Nice weather for the time of year, isn't it?"

Nope. It was always "How old is yours now? My Joe is seven months, he's got four teeth already." That's lovely. "And he's crawling now too" Hmm. That's great. "Last week he learned to abseil whilst solving complex algebra." Really?

It struck me that everyone was sizing up one another's offspring and working out if their child was out-performing the others in the key stages of development. Maybe I did it too. I probably did, but I've never really worried if another child was crawling or walking a little sooner than mine. After all, it's not likely they're going to grow up never having learned to walk, is it? They'll do it when they're good and ready, so don't fret about it.

If you're going to be heading into a world of mum chats, you may find a little preparation can help you hold your own.

Lazy dad's guide to parenting books

Do you remember all those parenting books your partner may, or may not have read. I guess you didn't read them either? No, I'm afraid flicking through the pages for twenty seconds whilst engrossed in a Fast and the Furious film doesn't really count. I'm not judging you. I didn't read much of them either.

Many, although not all mums, will be well versed in these books and the different methods of bringing up a baby available to the twenty-first century parent. You will find it much easier to hold down a conversation with a tea group of post-natal mums if you know your Gina Ford from your Jo Frost and that Dr Spock didn't have pointy ears and come from Vulcan.

But I'm looking after a baby, you say? I can't even sit on the toilet in peace - when am I ever going to read about how to be a better parent? The good news is that you don't have to. I'm going to give you a quick bluffers guide to parenting books so you can chat with the mums without making an idiot of yourself. Let's face it, you don't want to be known as a rubbish dad just because you confused Gina Ford with the woman who sang 'Ooh Aah...Just a Little Bit' at the Eurovision Song Contest.

Gina Ford

Gina Ford is 'The Queen of the Routine' and her bestselling
parenting guide 'The Contented Little Baby Book' sold a
formidable half a million copies. Her approach is a strict
regime for both parent and child, in which she micro-
manages your day into five-minute slots with set feeding
times for meals and naps. You can easily spot the Fordites.
They'll be the mums glancing at the time and performing
synchronized pushchair displays at the exact same time each
day. Honestly, sometimes you think you're in The Stepford
Wives, such is the robotic precision of Ford's advice.

I'm not criticizing her methods though. God, no. Not after
she almost sued mumsnet for publishing some rather
hostile comments about her approach to parenting. She is
controversial though and her methods have been compared
to training a dog. But you have to weigh that against the
parents who are finally sleeping through the night thanks to
Ford's policy of controlled crying.

Gina Ford is parenting Marmite - a menace to some and
a godsend to others. I had a look at 'The Contented Little
Baby Book' reviews on Amazon.co.uk. To date, she has had

600 'Gina saved my life' five-star reviews vs 300 'avoid at all costs' one-star reviews, so for every parent who threw her book in a charity shop in disgust there are two parents who will sing her praises.

Penelope Leach

That's Professor Penelope Leach to you. She suggests you discard parenting 'by the book', which is slightly ironic because, yes of course she does have a book. 'Your Baby & Child' encourages you to empathise with your baby and try taking their point of view. What does this mean? Well, only that all babies are different. They are all little individuals and that you can't treat them all alike with a rigid parenting style.

KAPOW! Take that Gina Ford. Leach goes so far as to say that letting your baby cry could give them brain damage. And she has science on her side. When a baby cries, it produces cortisol, otherwise known as stress and too much of this can be toxic. So, what do you do? Be aware of your child's needs and be patient, very patient. If your baby is happy, the more you will enjoy their company.

Tracy Hogg

Popularly known as the Baby Whisperer, Tracy Hogg claims to understand the secret language of babies. I guess calling her the Dr Doolittle of babies doesn't instil the same confidence in parents. No, I don't think she whispers to horses too. That's a different book altogether. The baby whisperer advocates a simple process of EASY (Eat,

Activity, Sleep, You time). What this means is that you feed your baby as soon as she wakes up, after which you'll play with her, stimulate her mind and when she gets ready to sleep again (without feeding) then you get some 'me time'.

I don't see any time allocated to doing the laundry, clearing the dishes or cooking a meal so I can only presume by 'me time' she means 'me running about frantically doing all the chores before the baby wakes up'. Some claim her methods can lead to calmer parenting, since you don't have a rigid timetable to adhere to, but when your child asks to be fed at 2am, 4am and 6am you may find yourself reaching for the 'let them cry, I need to sleep' philosophy of Gina Ford.

Jo Frost

You will probably know Jo under her pro-wrestling name, 'Supernanny'. She is the ballsy Mary Poppins on the telly who gets air dropped into the parenting equivalent of The Battle of the Somme each week. Her tactic is the 'naughty step' where children get a warning if they misbehave, but if they carry on they have to sit on a step - one minute for every year of their age, and then apologise.

What about babies? Despite her reputation as a parenting superweapon, Supernanny Jo focuses on surrounding your infant with love and attention and, like Leach, warns of the long-term affects of children brought up with minimal care. Learn to recognise your baby's body language and respond to her needs. She's big on cuddles, since touch is the first sense to develop and advises you don't make a habit of keeping the TV on, since it distracts your baby's attention from playing.

Boobs

You know your life has changed when you notice a woman's exposed nipple and find yourself thinking 'That must be handy. I wish I had boobs'...

I'm sure breast feeding is sore, often painful and frequently embarassing when you get a rude look for using your breasts for what nature intended, but it is convenient. Preparing a formula bottle is a drag. Wash the bottle, sterilise the bottle, boil the water, mix the powder and hot water, cool the milk. It takes a great deal of time and frankly, babies aren't exactly known for their patience are they? So, you need to plan all this ahead by about 20 minutes so the milk is precisely the correct temperature when she wants to drink it, or throw it all back up over you, depending on her mood.

Boob wars

There's a lot of politics around breast feeding. It's as complicated and fraught with opinions as bombing a small Middle Eastern country. I think of it as boob wars. I've lost you, haven't I? I didn't mean boob wars literally. You're daydreaming of topless women in an enthusiastic pillow fight, aren't you? Yeah, me too, I can't help it. But wait, this is a serious business.

Should your partner breast feed? Why won't the baby latch on? Has the baby drank enough? Where can you breast feed? Do you really have to put a sack over your baby's head as you feed them? Is it ok to feed them to sleep? It really is a minefield.

The benefits are irrefutable - it really is magical stuff. Indiana Jones spent an entire film chasing around looking for the elixir of life, but mothers milk is the real deal. Did you know a mother's nipple communicates with her baby's saliva and produces milk that meets the dietary needs of the child? It's simply extraordinary that a mother can provide every drop of water, food and nutrition her baby needs.

As a dad, your role is pretty much limited to fetching your other half the occasional glass of water (no hot drinks – too dangerous), or passing a cloth to preserve what's left of her modesty and fending off perverts.

Yet, despite the benefits, by the time a baby reaches three months only seventeen per cent of mothers exclusively breastfeed their child.

Why? Well, it comes down to the breast vs bottle debate:

Breast	Bottle
Great for mother/baby bonding	Have you ever seen a baby chew a bottle teat in half?
It's always available	What if there's a zombie apocalypse and the shop runs out of formula?
Mothers milk is chock full of immunity antibodies for the baby and can prevent breast cancer in mum	Shame on you for bottle feeding your baby! Oh, the tap didn't work? He couldn't latch on? I guess that's alright then
Not allowed to drink gin	Make mine a double!
It's free	Bottle steriliser, milk powder and the rest adds up to £££
Not allowed to eat shell-fish	Prawn cocktail anyone?

There is, of course, expressing. Your infant has all the benefits of breast feeding without the social awkwardness of a nipple spraying milk all over a strangers semi-skimmed latte. Well, perhaps, but again, it's alright for dad, but what if you're a mum returned to work? If it's awkward to conceal your modesty whilst breast feeding in a cafe, imagine what it's like sitting in meetings with your boob attached to a suction pump, making violent slurpy noises like you're nose deep in a McDonalds banana milkshake, as your boss discusses important corporate matters.

Obviously your partner would express somewhere more private, but where? Does she find an empty meeting room, shove a chair under the door handle and hope no one bursts in? That's pretty much what my wife had to do. When she asked her boss where she could find a room with a locked door so she could pump milk, he suggested using the disabled toilet. Now, ask yourself this, if someone prepared your lunch on a toilet seat, would you eat it?

Man boobs

I once foolishly suggested to my wife that I would breast feed, if I could, believing it to be as possible as growing a pouch and bouncing down the street. Here's some news. It is possible for men to lactate milk. What! Really? Yes, really. So, for god's sake, don't tell your wife. I still worry that my custard has been mixed with hormone replacement tablets.

In Anna Karenina, Tolstoy refers to a baby suckling on an Englishman for sustenance whilst on board a ship. The great Prussian explorer of South America, Alexander von Humboldt observed a man breast feeding his children after his wife fell ill. More recentlly, Agence France-Presse reported a Sri Lankan man nursing his baby daughters after his wife died in childbirth.

After the Second World War, there were extraordinary accounts of male prison camp survivors. Men who had suffered months of starvation. After they were released and received a normal diet, their doctors were stunned to notice these men were lactating milk from their nipples. It turned out their hormone-producing glands recovered more quickly than their livers, causing a spike in hormones. The liver would normally have regulated these hormones, but weakened by malnutrition, failed to do so. Interestingly, cirrhosis of the liver can have a similarly disruptive effect. They don't tell you that in rock and roll school, do they? Sex, drugs and lactating man boobs.

It is unusual though, unless you are an Indonesian fruit bat, which is unlikely admittedly. The male Dayak fruit bat appears to be the only species where the male spontaneously produces milk to feed its young. Although it has been observed in cats, goats and the occasional guinea pig.

So, men do potentially have the ability to breast feed their babies, but only in extreme cases. Unless you have been starved, suffered a massive Keith Richards liver cirrhosis, you're a minor character in a Tolstoy novel or happen to be an Indonesian fruit bat, your man boobs will run empty unless you consume enough medication to shame a Ukranian Olympic wrestler.

No peaking

Breast may be best but as a stay at home dad, I think we have established you'll be hitting the bottle. But, you can't escape - you're still going to find yourself in a world of boobs and breast feeding. You're going to need to know what's the social etiquette for a dad.

Well, the rules are certainly different. As a woman, conversations around leaking nipples, blocked ducts and swollen boobs are all fair game. As a mum, you can discuss feeding techniques, move the infant like this, squeeze your boob like that, offer tips, advice and share horror stories. As a dad, in a mum's world, you must not get involved in these conversations. If a mum has broccoli in her teeth, you might want to politely tell her, but if she is lactating milk into her infant's ear, or she's gushing the Okavanga Delta of milk all over the floor - for God's sake, LOOK AWAY NOW! Don't get involved. It can only end badly for you. You shouldn't even be looking. In fact, avoid any eye to boob contact whatsoever.

I find that a great deal of discretion and careful eye contact is required. It's not too difficult once you get used to it. Any kind of rummaging of clothing will usually prepare you to maintain strict eye contact and avoid any awkward wandering eyes. But the pressure is there in a way that women don't encounter. If a woman notices a fellow mum's nipple, it's without the potentially fraught social disaster of a dad doing so. As a chap, you feel like you're always one step away from being slapped around the chops and being branded a pervert.

And whatever you do, never, NEVER, under any circumstances tell a woman she has nice boobs and they're hardly droopy at all. Did I ever say that at nursery? Are you kidding? The mums would have lynched me with the nearest Jumberoo. Personally and I can't speak for every man, but the sight of a mother with her exposed nipple plugged into a small infants gob lacks any sort of sexual appeal whatsoever. And don't get me wrong, I love boobs. I really do.

Daddy's big day out

The temptation is to stay at home a lot. Why go out, when it's so much easer to stay at home where you have a safe environment for your baby to play, a high-chair, a fridge full of snacks, your milk and bottle steriliser to hand and a cot for nap time. But, there will come a time when you realise you're in danger of going bat-shit crazy and really need to leave the house.

Going out can be hard work. I'd pop Squeaky in her pushchair twice a day to get her to nap and pick up some supplies in the village. That was fine. Going out for longer can be a challenge. The easy option is to drive to someone's house. You can throw as much stuff as you like in the boot (change bag - check, booster seat - check, half her wardrobe - check, crate full of fruit and snacks - check, contents of medicine cabinet - check, kitchen sink - stop already!)

For the seriously hard-core, pioneering parent, getting on a train to explore town is a proper expedition. You think I'm exaggerating? When I told some mums at playgroup that I was taking my baby to London for the day, they stared at me - stunned and mouths agog. Anyone would think I was taking my offspring to a collapsed Japanese nuclear power facility.

Going out checklist:

1. Nappies (x5)
2. Wet wipes
3. Change mat
4. Bum cream
5. Change of clothes (x2)
5. Teething granules
6. Snacks
7. Sterilised milk bottles (x2)
8. Milk powder
9. Thermos of boiling water (for making milk)
10. Lunch (hers)

When you do venture out, an important decision will be choosing between taking the pushchair or using a baby carrier.

If it's a short trip of two to three hours then a baby carrier may be more convenient - you have greater agility and can more easily manage the crowds. We took our son to the Hockney exhibition at The Royal Academy when he was a baby and thanks to the baby carrier, he slept through the whole thing. Still, I couldn't overcome the feeling I was strapped to a pack of plastic explosive and any moment he'd wake up with an explosive scream and we'd flee the scene in a fit of apologies.

If you are going out all day then you will want to take the pushchair so you can put your baby down and give yourself a rest. There will be times when you may feel like a competitor in The World's Strongest Man, as you lug the pushchair up and down countless flights of stairs. Just remember, the upside is that you won't have to carry her very often and you can enjoy a coffee without the terrible hazard of a baby strapped to your stomach.

You will want to have some kind of plan of where you are going, when, where and how you are going to feed your baby and where your nearest change facilities are. The last thing you want is a child in meltdown because they are hungry and there's no room at the inn. Or worse still, they poop themselves in a screaming fit and out of desperation you try changing their nappy behind the discounted rail in Primark, before being escorted away by shop security. Tube stations don't have baby change facilities, typically neither do pubs or cafes. Instead, you want to know where to find your nearest museum, gallery, cinema, shopping centre, department store or failing all else, McDonalds. Parks are good too, but not in winter or between midday and 2pm near an office. Would you want to see the contents of a child's nappy whilst enjoying your well earned burrito, with extra pulled-pork? I didn't think so.

How did I get on? I was keen to check out the Cosmonaut exhibition at the Science Museum, so, I dusted off my travel card, refreshed the change bag and braved a trip on the London Underground with the pushchair. Was it a long journey? Not really, but it felt epic, especially when my daughter wouldn't stop crying unless I stood up and held her. That's not an easy feat when the tube is bouncing about like a high speed trampoline.

By the time we pulled into South Kensington I felt like I'd been wrestling a small, wild animal for the better part of an hour, whilst being catapulted to the moon and back. The exhibition incidentally was stunning. Everything from the Soviet lunar lander to Yuri Gagarin's uniform had been gathered and dusted off, having spent the intervening years squirreled away in secret labs and Russian oligarch's sheds.

Squeaky behaved after a placating dose of milk, but whenever I repeated these trips, she'd invariably cry unless I picked her up. Trust me, it's not easy to appreciate early photography or the designs of Da Vinci whilst your baby is more interested in exploring your nose.

When you're out and about, you must expect your typical routine to take a catastrophic kick in the knackers. Your baby won't eat at her usual time and her naps will probably be all over the shop. It's a new world for her and it's chock-full of distractions. You never realise how noisy the world is until you are pushing a sleeping baby around a public place - roads, public transport, don't get me started on coffee shops, they're all full of loud, random noises that as adults we've managed to tune out. You can't even get into a nice, peaceful lift without everything shouting at you.

"I'M OPENING NOW, NEARLY THERE! YES, YOU CAN GET IN NOW" shrieked the lift, it's doors gnashing and grinding like some terrible mechanical beast.

I gently shunted my pushchair back and forth to prevent Squeaky from waking.

The button for the second floor was pressed with a deafening BING!

"I'M IN A LIFT! I'M GOING TO GET CUT OFF! shouted one passenger at his phone. A retired couple bickered over whether the toasters could be found in the Electricals department, or as seemed more likely to me, in the Home section.

Squeaky was now awake and crying. Screw you lifts.

You might be thinking - bloody hell, that sounds more trouble than it's worth. Well, that's up to you. It isn't easy - there may be tears, you may be politely asked to leave if your child throws up over something expensive, but if you are prepared and manage your expectations of what you can expect to do, then you can enjoy your day out with an enormous sense of achievement and with minimal collateral damage.

Mums vs dads

A few months ago, I was chatting with a mum friend whilst we rocked our babies to sleep and I asked her what she thought about full-time dads.

"I'm not sure if my husband has the patience to look after the kids full-time" she confessed.

"To be honest, I doubt most men do." I think I surprised myself with my response. At the time I had been looking after Squeaky for some months and had survived, endured and yes, enjoyed the challenges of being a stay-at-home dad. But I wasn't inclined to disagree with this mum.

Perhaps she was right. Sure, dads can do the parenting but are we at a disadvantage? After all, an abundance of male testosterone is hardly helpful when looking after a baby. Are men more likely to lose their temper and struggle with their patience levels being stretched to breaking point? Are women just better physically and emotionally equipped to handle a baby?

By all accounts the European Union didn't seem to know either, so they commissioned some research and found that the first six weeks of maternity leave is pretty much about the female-only stuff – recovering from the birth and breastfeeding. Everything after then is just looking after children and can be done by mums and dads alike.

So, what qualities do you need to care for your baby? Well, patience obviously, meticulous preparation, strength of mind, ability to do endless loads of laundry and be willing to spend time with your child, reading to and playing with them. None of these skills strike me as exclusively female.

What about breast is best? Well, that may be true, but is it really a reason for dad to step aside? According to unicef only one per cent of families exclusively breastfeed their baby for the full six months recommended by the World Health Organisation.

What about dads having too much unhelpful aggression due to testosterone? This is where things get really interesting. There is evidence that suggests testosterone levels fall in men when they become fathers. A study at the University of Michigan found that a crying infant can trigger a drop in testosterone levels in men. The lower testosterone then makes dads less aggressive and more able to empathise with their child. In a nut shell, nature rewires dad's brain so he's more likely to think his child is upset because they need comforting, rather than because his child is a noisy little sod, hell-bent on ruining season six of Game of Thrones.

Nature may be giving dads a helping hand in other respects too. Professor Samuel Weiss at the University of Calgary's Hotchkiss Brain Institute discovered that becoming a father may have a transformative effect on the brain cells. Weiss discovered that when male mice interact with their new-born babies, they develop new brain cells in the part of the brain responsible for their sense of smell and memory - which may explain those unexpected daddy super powers.

Can dads make better parents than mums? Well, I have no interest in provoking every woman on the planet to want to kick me in the nuts, but I will say this. In my humble opinion, there's no reason why dads can't be as caring, resourceful and patient as mums, given the opportunity.

.

Daddy playgroup

A t some point, it's nice to have a conversation with another bloke. It's not easy though and finding other chaps to talk to during those long days of childcare is easier said than done when all your friends are cocooned away in their offices and there isn't another full-time dad in sight.

You have to use a bit of imagination. I missed talking about music so I'd head to the new record shop in the nearest town, buy something interesting but inexpensive like a slightly worn Graham Nash LP and chat on with the proprietor about gigs, favourite musicians and how you can make a living selling second hand records (barely, I think). It was the same at the butcher's. He's been in the village for years so we sauntered down memory lane awhile, remembering former headmasters, village drunks and debating what makes a good sausage.

Hanging out with the butcher was fine, but what I wanted to do was meet other dads in a similar situation to me. I was curious to discover how other men had experienced being a stay-at-home dad and how they'd found bringing up their baby. The problem was we dads appear to be a rare breed, not so much near extinction, more a colourful exception to the rule, like the lonely chinchilla in the pet shop surrounded by gerbils and rabbits.

Now, don't get me wrong, it's not like dads are excluded from normal playgroups. They're not (mostly) but they are run by women, for women. Most have the decency to call themselves something inclusive like 'Toddler group, Peek-a-Boo baby, Baby and Toddler group, Quackers or Sunshine'. Yet, to find these places you'll end up using the netmums website and many groups appear less than welcoming to fathers: 'Mums & toddlers, Bump and baby, Mums coffee morning, Mums playgroup, First time Mums, Mum and baby group'.

I looked online. I live on the edge of London, a cosmopolitan and open minded city of several million people, I reasoned there must be tens of thousands of dads like me, and dozens, if not hundreds of events, societies and playgroups geared towards stay at home dads. I was wrong, or at least I was mostly wrong. On the plus side of being mostly wrong, it also meant I was a little bit right. Sometimes, that's good enough.

There was one. One playgroup in all of London that was specifically for dads - in the womble conservation zone of Wimbledon.

'Dads'n'little uns' looked like a typical playgroup at first, held in a church hall as these things typically are, but inside it was different. Eight or nine dads stood around, sipping cups of tea whilst holding or looking over their infants. A welcoming cup of tea was much appreciated. 'Where have you come from?' I was asked. About an hour away, near the end of the Metropolitan line, I explained, to quietly stunned faces. 'I think that might be a new record' one commented. 'Nah, not quite, dya remember that bloke used to come from Highbury?'

A chap called Bill introduced himself as he poured the tea and put out the biscuits. "We've been going for more than ten years now. It was set up by a journalist who was home looking after the kids and realised there was nothing available for dads. So, we're a bit different to other playgroups where the emphasis is on the kids. We're more about the dads, a support group if you like, somewhere you can get out the house and have a chat with someone in a similar situation.'

Our conversation was interrupted, as they typically are when you're a parent. I withdrew to give Squeaky her morning bottle feed amidst a low level background hubbub of reasonably calm, but exuberent toddlers. I listened in on the nearest conversation. 'I've been fighting - JOE! GIVE THE BABY HER BALL BACK PLEASE - hit me hard, my nose is pretty messed up.' Gosh, I thought. I had wondered if dads talked about something other than the state of their babies nappies but I hadn't expected the tipping of oestrogen to testosterone in the room to be so dramatic. 'Better now though (cough) bit of a sniffle but that's about it'. Oh, I thought as I realised he was talking about fighting off a cold, not walloping someone in a boozer.

I got chatting to Tim, whose son was a similar age to my daughter. As we sat in the ball pit, sharing dad stories, it became clear how important this group was. Tim had gone along to one of the regular Saturday meet ups for dads, held at the local children's centre - but quickly realised he didn't have anything in common with the other fathers.

"They all worked full-time and only had to look after the baby for an hour or so at the weekend - but they all sat there and moaned about how hard it was and fretted about how to hold the baby properly. I just wanted to tell them to get a grip for God's sake. I found I had more in common with the mums, but even then it's awkward when they start discussing, y'know, gynaecological stuff".

Something I'd noticed along my baby travels was a sense of prevailing guilt. Now most mums I know feel guilty. Guilty about not breast feeding, guilty for not providing the best meal for their child, guilty for wanting a moment to themselves and - wow - they really crucify themselves for returning to work and dropping their baby off into childcare.

What was interesting was the number of dads who felt like this too. Tim off work for twelve weeks with his son. "I love it, I love spending time with my son but I'm half way through my time now and I still feel like I'm an imposter, I can't give him the time I want to. I'm not a proper stay at home dad".

As far as I could tell, every father's circumstance was different. There were full time dads on a career break, one who'd lost his job and another on shared parental leave. There were dads on shift work, working nights or weekends and caring for junior for a day or two whilst mum worked, as well as a few overseas dads with high-flying wives who had taken on full-time daddy duties. Yet, it appeared to me, we all had something in common. Having spent eight years running 'Dads'n'little uns', Bill had spotted it too.

"It's more relaxed isn't it? The kids are more calm when they're surrounded by dads and you won't find any cliques here. Everyone looks out for one another and no one judges you if you have a different approach to bringing up your kid." He had a point, but what did it mean? Can dads make better parents than mums? It was a controversial thought and I can imagine a mum reading this in astonishment and thinking, my husband can't even butter his own toast, let alone look after our baby.

I wasn't sure what to think until I had lunch with my sister, Eve, a couple of weeks later. Her maternity leave coincided with my own time off work and we'd meet up every week or so, have a chat and let our babies poke each other in the face for a bit. I'm going to take a slight diversion first because I have to mention the meal that was set down before us, if for no other reason than it may have been the least appetising thing to appear on a plate since Mr Creosote exploded at the end of his meal in Monty Python's 'The Meaning of Life'.

Their speciality was hotdogs (which must be a low bar to set yourself as a restaurant) but did they serve their sausage in a bun? Oh no. The choice was a waffle or a pancake. The waiter recommended the waffle and served our drinks in a jam jar, of which he was unnecessarily enthusiastic. The Coney island hotdog was served in what I can only describe as a state of distress, sliced and splayed as if some medieval torturer had mutilated and abandoned this unfortunate sausage on top of a waffle, spattered with ketchup, like a low budget horror movie.

Luckily, the conversation was a welcome distraction. "The dads are probably more calm than a typical group of mums," explained my sister, "but it's a self selecting group, isn't it?"

I hadn't thought of that. In a nutshell, the sort of men who choose to look after their infants full-time are unlikely to represent all types of men. Yes, there were professional golfers, cameramen, IT specialists and teachers, but the point is, you're probably not going to find a hedge fund manager from Goldman Sachs changing nappies.

A fellow dad told me that he was at dinner once with friends and they were discussing parenting. One father, who is a big shot in the city, stood up and loudly pronounced "I don't change nappies! I don't cook meals! Those are my rules!"

He was an investment banker. I've nothing against people who are investment bankers. Some of them are very nice people indeed, but it's a tough industry that attracts fiercely competitive men. Alpha males who will prefer to prove their worth in the battlefield of money and bring home the loot.

The sort of dads who would prefer to balance their career with spending time with their babies will be a different breed, less aggressive perhaps, calmer and maybe less extrovert by nature. If every dad was legally obliged to take care of their baby for a few months - like National Service, except with nappies instead of a rifle, then no doubt you'd find playgroups a frenzy of men desperately pitting their babies small accomplishments against another.

"Jeremy started walking last week".

"Daisy is six months old and doing backflips now."

"Jennifer is nine months and had her first driving lesson."

"Well, David has a BMW 3 series."

"Argh, my child's better than yours!" Whallop!

Can I watch some telly?

I never imagined I'd be sitting around all day, watching telly, but I was looking forward to getting past season two of Breaking Bad and re-watching Twin Peaks. How did that go, do you think?

Well, the truth is, being at home alone with your baby for potentially twelve hours at a stretch, you do have some time. There are gaps between the relentless frenzy of milk prepping, bum wiping and making meals. There you are, sat on the floor, your child crawling over your lap and you're all out of nursery rhymes.

Treat yourself, switch off CBeebies which is humming away in the background and watch something you want to watch because trust me, you don't have very long before your child wrestles complete control of the television away from you. You'll need to be prepared for this because children's TV isn't the world of saggy old cloth cats and sock puppets like when you were small.

Tots TV

Postman Pat is still around but his amiable bumbling
has now degenerated into full-blown incompetence. To
my knowledge, he has lost a cow, two robots, a fruit bat,
a horse, a movie reel, a block of ice, a teddy bear and one
giant cake containing a policeman. Pat must have a terrific
union. And it's not like Pat doesn't have the resources. He
has not one - but two vans, a motorbike with side-car (for
the cat), a helicopter, a snowmobile and a quad bike. No
wonder the price of stamps went up. If Greendale was on the
coast, I'd expect Postman Pat would have his own nuclear
submarine which - due to Pat's rampant negligence and
some faulty wiring by local handyman, Ted Glenn - would
have transformed Pencaster into Chernobyl. Interestingly,
there was a new Postman Pat movie where Pat was replaced
by an evil Pat-shaped robot called the Patbot 3000. Maybe,
Sarah Connor was right after all, except Skynet's robots
don't look like Arnold Schwarzenegger, they're all Patbots.

The Teletubbies are back too and are even more weird and confusing than before. I was watching the show with Squeaky and Padawan one morning, when my son asked me if the Teletubbies were children, or grown ups.

"Do they play like children", I asked him.

"Yes", he replied.

"Do they talk like babies?" I asked.

"Yes, they do, daddy."

"So, they must be children." I reasoned.

"But why do they have babies" he asked.

"What?", I replied.

Right enough, the Teletubbies now have babies - which raises all sorts of questions. I like to think I'm an open minded parent. I don't have a problem with a commune of sexually ambiguous bear-people raising children together - I really don't. But the Teletubbies appear to have the collective IQ of an economy sausage roll and I seriously question their ability to grow dandelions, let alone raise children.

I've never much cared for The Little Princess. I found her 'charming impulsiveness' brattish and obnoxious, but I have a great deal more sympathy for her now I have figured out the profoundly peculiar nature of her upbringing. If you are unfamiliar with this show, it's about a young girl who lives in a slightly shabby castle that really ought to be handed over to the National Trust. The princess lives there, with her father and mother (who call themselves the King and Queen) as well as people claiming to be the General and the Prime Minister. I've come to the inevitable conclusion that the castle is some sort of combined child and adult psychiatric unit and the characters who live there have been sectioned under The Mental Health Act.

Apart from Maid, who I suspect may be the one in charge and dosing the soup with mild sedatives. Each and every character exhibits some, or all of the symptoms of psychotic behaviour, including hallucinations, false perceptions and beliefs, bizarre behaviour and delusions. The Little Princess really ought to be in a dedicated juvenile centre, under closer supervision. I am concerned her repeated tantrums may have been misdiagnosed as Attention Defecit Disorder and she may be a full-blown schizophrenic.

Topsy and Tim are a curious pair of children. We are told they are twins, but they don't behave like it. Twins are chaos to the power of ten. Twins will run in opposite directions to gain a strategic advantage over their exhausted parents. They will take turns to sleep in order to wear down their parents and maximise their opportunity to shove their hands in the birthday cake.

In fact, Topsy and Tim are not twins - it says so on the credits, they're not even related. It's possible they may be part of a covert mind control experiment though. What four year old do you know would say 'Sprouts for snack time, mummy? You do spoil us! May I have extra broccoli please?'

Which brings me to the kingpin of kids telly. Believe me, I like Justin Fletcher. His old fashioned style of clowning and vaudeville is a refreshing change from the cynical post-David Brent world of embarrassment comedy. It doesn't bother me that Justin has the same slightly gelatinous face as David Cameron.

What concerns me is the extent of his ambition. You can't escape from Justin Fletcher, he practically owns CBeebies. On any given day, you can find Fletcher on Justin's House, GiggleBiz or Something Special. He's even there when you can't see him as he voices characters in Tiny Tumble, Doodles, Tweenies, Finley the Fire Engine, CBeebies' Boo!, Shaun the Sheep and Timmy Time.

What really finished Justin for us, was when I'd arranged a day out with my wife and we'd packed both kids off to nursery. It was a rare and precious thing, having the day together, just the two of us. Amy expressed an interest in seeing the production of The Railway Children, but who was making a special guest appearance as Mr Perks? Justin bloody Fletcher, that's who!

Grown up TV

The truth is you can sit and watch a bit of telly. The problem is, you will struggle to make sense of what is going on. Why?

Well, firstly, don't forget you have a small, demanding and lovable ball of energy rolling about, getting herself into all kinds of mischief. You will be constantly distracted.

The second thing is that your child makes an awful lot of noise, squeaking and gurgling with little pause for breath. So, whilst you can (more or less) watch a show, you certainly can't hear it, or rather you can only hear bits of it. You know how your DVDs always come with special extras? The optional voice-over where the director explains why he used a particular camera angle, or shares an anecdote about how Tom Hanks farted and they had to dub it out? Well, it's a bit like that, but instead of the director, imagine it's a hungry orangatan in the homeware department of Selfridges and everything's smeared with bananas.

Let me give you an example. This is how my attempt to spend some quality time with coffee quaffing Dale Cooper and the inhabitants of Twin Peaks played out:

"You'll recall that on the day of her death Laura Palmer wrote in her (burble) the following (Waah!)...Harry, if you would, when I give the word, would you please (Beh beh beh) each of the names we've written on the (BEEP! "mulberry bush on a cold and frosty morning"), all of whom had a direct connection with (BOING BOING CRASH!! Small avalaunche of plastic toys)..bucket of rocks up near me where I can get at them ... and would you please wear the kitchen (Boing boing! My name is bear - what's your name? My favourite colour is)...pass the donuts."

Confusing, isn't it? Although, it must be said as groundbreaking and compelling as Twin Peaks is (and it really is, even twenty years later) it was always bloody confusing. You can partially solve this audio problem by putting the subtitles on. Even before having kids, I watched the entire five seasons of Baltimore crime drama, The Wire and most of the Sopranos with the subtitles on, due to the characters excessive mumbling and incomprehensible dialects. Of course, for the subtitles to be helpful you still need to concentrate long enough to read the words on the screen, which isn't easy when a small someone is abseiling down your face and using your nose as a handy crampon.

Perhaps I was too ambitious attempting to watch Twin Peaks. It would certainly be rather easier to watch something with less dialogue or a more simple plot. Have you ever seen the film 'The Social Network'? The script is so tightly packed with dialogue, you wonder when Jesse Eisenberg and Andrew Garfield will come up for air. This is exactly the type of film you should abandon any hope of watching whilst on daddy duty. You'll probably have more luck watching a big action movie where you don't need to worry too much about missing the particular reason Jason Statham is trying to garrot the big man in a sweaty vest.

Sports might work too. The long lazy gaps in a cricket match might lend itself to looking after a small infant. The problem is you never know when your child will decide to wreak havoc/howl at the moon/shit themselves.

You are likely to discover that your child has an uncanny ability to time their outburst precisely two seconds before the all important goal/break point/knockout punch. So, if you don't already have a Tivo box, get one. You will be needing that rewind button.

Baby gym

You may be wondering, as a stay at home dad, am I going to turn to flab like some great cheese burger chomping walrus? I don't have time to run or go the gym anymore - how am I going to keep myself fit? Especially after a long day sitting around eating cake with yummy mummys. All I can say to that is 'Ha ha ha! You're kidding right?'

You'll be amazed at the number of calories you burn off, running around after your little one. You're constantly on your feet, prepping milk bottles, doing washing up, picking her up to stop her crying, running upstairs for more nappies and marching around the block with the pushchair. It really never ends. I lost about ten pounds looking after my daughter without even trying.

But if you really want to go running, what do you do? Well, you have two options - push her or carry her. You're welcome to try either, but I'm not sure I'd recommend it.

I had never intended to take my daughter running, but fourteen minutes before the nursery closed, Amy rang to tell me the traffic was in meltdown and could I collect our son. I gathered my wits, strapped on the baby harness, popped my daughter on my chest (11 minutes and counting), shoved my shoes on, grabbed my keys and fell out the door (10 minutes left). I started at a gentle jog, steadying my daughter to prevent any aggressive jiggling.

I'll confess, I'm not a natural runner and my legs manically flip-flopped along, propelling me in a somewhat unsteady fashion along the pavement. Leisurely dog walkers dragged their beloved pets out of harms way as I passed (six minutes left). Rather quickly, my breath grew increasingly laboured and my pace dropped back to a brisk march. I know, for gods sake Tindale, you've only been running five minutes - what's wrong with you? Well, it's not easy, running with ten pounds of bouncing baby strapped to your chest.

And did I mention, it was winter? The cold air tore through my throat like premium grade sandpaper. I passed the shops, fell up the hill and down the other side (4 minutes until closing). Past the library, shambled past the pub, looked longingly at the other pub (2 minutes), down the lane (one minute) and almost threw up over the entrance to the nursery as the clock struck six.

Or you can run with a pushchair. There is a group of post-natal mums (and maybe the occasional post-natal dad) called 'Buns of Steel' who meet regularly to run around parks with their pushchairs. You just need to be a bit careful though. You may not have noticed but pushchairs are not half as stable as they might seem and pavements aren't as flat as you'd expect. The pavement outside my house looks like it's endured a minor earthquake. Inject some high-octane foot power into the equation and you're looking at rearranging your nose on the tarmac, or worse still, your child's. So, if you're still sure you want to break a sweat with your pushchair, make sure its in a park with a nice smooth surface to prevent unexpected facial realignment.

If you are more of a gym Jim, but can't find the time to keep up your membership, then maybe you should try looking at your darling child in a new light. Yes, they are the love of your life, yes, you would do anything for them, yes of course she is beautiful.

Don't forget though, she also weighs as much as a sack of potatoes and is well suited for weight-lifting. After all, she's getting bigger and heavier with each passing week, which is more or less the same as slipping a couple of kilos on to your weight-lifting bar. Before you attempt any of the following, use your noggin and make sure she is sturdy and strong enough to support her head and enjoy a little bouncing about with daddy.

1. Bench press with baby. Lie on your back and hold on to your child with your hands firmly gripping them around their armpit. Then gently lift them vertically up and down. Bend your knees to focus on your biceps. Or keep your legs flat on the floor to work your stomach muscles too. A terrific and versatile exercise.

2. Stand up with your feet firmly planted on the floor. Then bend your knees, drop into a squat position, pick up your child and stand up. The closer you hold your child to your chest, the less strain you will put on your back muscles, so adjust to what works for you. Repeat.

3. Why not incorporate a few push ups with changing your infant's nappy? It will help you create a workout routine as well as a stinky incentive to push further than you expected.

4. Use your baby carrier whilst catching up on daily chores. You will be amazed how much energy you use up whilst hanging the laundry with ten kilos of baby strapped to your chest.

5. Pick up your baby and walk up and down the stairs ten times.

6. Get on your hands and knees and lift your bum in the air (a downward dog in yoga). You have now created a bridge and impromptu play area for your toddler to crawl beneath

7. Lay on your back, bend your knees and lift your child on to your legs. Whilst holding their hands, lift your legs up and down.

8. Lunges. Pick your baby up. Jump your feet apart with straight legs

Nursery rhymes

You might not have realised it but you are now part of a double act and like all great double acts - Morecambe and Wise, the Two Ronnies, Ant and Dec and those films Clint Eastwood made with an orangatan - there is a large one and a small one, a very funny one and a much less funny one and you are both totally inseparable.

In your case, your side-kick is also your audience. The good news is that your audience is easily impressed. Let's face it, no one else smiles when you juggle one satsuma. The bad news is that your one-person audience is also impatient, wildy unpredictable and prone to heckling.

Nursery rhymes are a timeless and bullet-proof way of entertaining your little one. You may not realise it but you will probably have the words to Old McDonald, Row the boat, Wheels on the bus, Hickory dickory dock, Twinkle twinkle little star and Humpty dumpty burned into your memory from your own childhood. You might need a refresher course in remembering the hand movements that accompany the songs though. Any local playgroup will fill in the gaps for you, or there's always YouTube.

There does come a time though, where you can't bear to sing another verse of Old McDonald and you are sick of twinkling little bloody stars. I'd been trying to rock my daughter to sleep for some twenty minutes and had reached my seventeenth verse of Twinkle, twinkle, little star before I started improvising. Don't blame me. It was Row the boats fault. Did you know that the lovely genteele rhyme of messing about on the river has been changed and modernised to include screaming and crocodiles, like some high-octane Michael Bay movie? It got my goat, it really did, but after I'd calmed down and my wife had patiently explained that it didn't matter, I realised that anyone can have a go at making up nursery rhymes. I'm not saying I was any good but it entertained the both of us, although I suspect she tolerated my musings rather than approved of them.

I should explain, this was around the time British astronaut, Tim Peake was orbiting the earth in the International Space Station and David Bowie had recently deceased. Incidentally, it helps if you sing like Liam Gallagher and pronounce 'vacation' as 'vacatiaaaaan'.

Twinkle, twinkle, international space station
Where do you go on your vacation
What's the world like when it's snowy

Do you also miss David Bowie
Twinkle, twinkle, international space station
Where do you go on your vacation

It didn't stop there. I spent so long marching around the village with the pushchair that I developed my own theme tune - loosely based on the 1970's blaxploitation tune, Pusher Man by Curtis Mayfield:

I'm your mama, I'm your daddy
If it's smelly, change your nappy
I'm your doctor, I'm a fella
Is it time for your bonjela
You know me, I'm your friend
Your main boy, thick and thin
I'm your pusherman
I'm your pusherman...

I attempted, but swiftly abandoned a hip-hop re-inpretation of Wee Willie Winkie (well, he does rap at the windows, doesn't he?) Instead, I took on Old Mcdonald had a farm. What can I say? It's not as easy as it looks but it helped pass the time:

Michael Eavis had a farm
Ee-i-ee-i-oh
And on that farm he had Radiohead
Ee-i-ee-i-oh
Karma Police here
Karma Police there

Here Karma Police
There Karma Police
Everywhere Karma Police

Michael Eavis had a farm
Ee-i-ee-i-oh
And on that farm he had Lady Gaga
Ee-i-ee-i-oh
Pokerface here
Pokerface there
Here Pokerface
There Pokerface
Everywhere Pokerface

Michael Eavis had a farm
Ee-i-ee-i-oh
And on that farm he had the Rolling Stones
Ee-i-ee-i-oh
Satisfaction here
Satisfaction there
Here Satisfaction
There Satisfaction
Everywhere Satisfaction

Please feel free to make up your own verses. If enough of us
do it, we might even get invited to perform at Worthy Farm
next June.

Zen and the art of dadding

You might have realised by now that any expectations you may of had of putting your feet up amidst an idyllic life of biscuit dunking whilst looking after your beloved baby have evaporated in a great cloud of screaming bedlam.

There's very little calm in looking after a baby. I'm not saying it's without its rewards. Spending six months with my baby daughter was a frequent delight. I would compare it to feeling like I was falling in love, again and again.

Still, you can't avoid the fact that chaos is your constant companion. Your life is a tumbling cavalcade of broken nights sleep, and navigating seemingly random outbursts of crying and tantrums. You're so far removed from relaxed, you no longer remember what it feels like.

When I attempt to explain parenting to someone who doesn't have kids, I compare it to a rollercoaster. There are terrific highs that fill your heart with joy but before you know it, you're in a steep and downward spin and you can't get off. Sometimes I imagine myself in the eye of a tornado. You can grab a moment of exquisite calm and tranquillity but you can't ever escape the fact you're surrounded by turmoil that threatens to engulf you at any moment.

There was one morning in particular when my darling child was crying and screaming with the stamina of a long distance runner. Blood pulsed through my brain at a pace of knots and the dull throb in my head upgraded to a full blown brass band. Worse still, the brass band was in London Zoo and the monkeys were conducting the whole, horrendous cacaphony of noise. I flung a coat on my little monster and clicked her into the pushchair. She couldn't scream any louder, could she? Oh, she could and she did. We shot out the front door, banking the pushchair on two wheels as we took the bend at a rapid pace. On, I marched. Still, she screamed and screamed and SCREAMED. Then there was a quiet pop and my head exploded.

It was messy. I won't lie. There was blood and brain tissue over the pavement, my parietal lobe made a terrible stain on a Ford Mondeo. My occipital lobe ended up half-way up a tree and I was definitely going to need to handwash my jumper.

The important thing to remember, however bad it gets and you can be quite sure you will lose your mind at times, it won't always be like this. I can confidently predict with 99.9% certainty that your brain will not explode like an early David Cronenbourg movie and you will not have to redecorate the walls and ceiling.

You're probably expecting some practical advice on how to stop your baby crying. Well, I'm sorry to disappoint you. This is not that book.

You need another parenting book. You know, the sort. Let your baby cry and they will learn to stop crying, Let your baby cry and you will traumatise them and give them brain damage. Give your child finger food to encourage their hand-eye co-ordination. Give your child finger food and they might choke. They should sleep in your room as long as possible to nurture love and confidence. They must not sleep in your room after six months or they will grow up hopelessly dependent. You know the drill.

I don't know how to stop your baby going mental. It's just what babies do.

Besides, I'm not talking about a calmer baby. I'm talking about you. Are you feeling calm? Probably not, but the fact is you will be more mindful of those fleeting calm moments because of the time you spend with your child. What do I mean? Only that it's impossible to know true calm until you have experienced total, complete and utter chaos.

Do you remember what it was like to have a cup of tea without someone shouting or crawling over you? You probably took the moment for granted and idly wondered about (a) what to have for dinner (b) sex (c) what's on telly (d) do we have any biscuits (e) more sex.

If I get a moment to drink a cup of tea in peace, I don't find myself thinking of anything at all. So much of my time and personal head-space is absorbed by the immediate needs of Squeaky that my brain comes to a great shuddering stop, given the opportunity. It's like a safety valve has gone off, the knots in my shoulders loosen ever so slightly, my brain stops spinning and I can actually taste my tea, rather than throw it down my gullet whilst dashing between the washing machine and my daughter.

Zen is a word that's tossed about a great deal in our world. There is perhaps a misconception that it's about relaxing. Sitting cross legged on some mountain plateau or ashram, chanting 'om' without wondering where your child has hidden all the little blue detergent cups because you really need to do a load of laundry.

Zen is about being in the moment. Not carelessly dwelling on the past. Not constantly thinking about what else you should be doing, nor planning what you will do later in the week. Instead, you are just focussed on the here and now.

Looking after a baby doesn't give you much opportunity to think about anything, except meeting their needs at this precise moment in time. Your baby doesn't care what happened five minutes ago or what you might do in ten minutes. They only care that you play with them, change them, feed them - right now.

Every now and then you must plan a little, y'now make sure you have her lunch sorted or her bottle prepped when you need it. You don't have the luxury of disengaging entirely. For the most part though, I noticed how my mind was constantly in the moment, with all the beauty, hardship and vividness this brings.

If you don't find yourself 'in the moment' because you can't stop thinking of the great list of jobs that need doing - her clothes need sorting, meals need cooking, laundry to be hung, then stop. If your child is just becoming an obstacle to getting other things done, then stop. Caring for your baby is a full-time job. Well, not really. If you were at work, you'd be doing shorter hours, permitted to stop for lunch or a cup of tea and you can take a piss without someone shouting at you. No? Then you really need to get a new job. The point is, if you can get to the end of the day and have successfully fed and watered your child without breaking her, or having a nervous breakdown then you have achieved enough already. If you also managed to put the washing machine on and hang the laundry then you are a bloody star. Cooked a meal? Easy, superhero, what are you made of? You're going to make the rest of us look bad.

If you're still struggling to put that list of jobs out of your mind, then leave the house. It's much easier to focus on your child when everything else is out of sight and out of mind. Or agree with yourself that you'll do your best to prep a meal or tackle the washing up, but set aside an hour for playtime with your child and absolutely nothing else. Switch your phone off and learn to enjoy stacking blocks or rolling about on the floor with your child. It's why you are doing this, after all. Besides, your child is less likely to be upset and angry if you are enjoying your time with her.

Baby gadgets and stuff

If you find yourself wandering about a department store, semi comatose due to sleep deprivation and resembling a minor character from George A. Romero's classic zombie film 'Dawn of the Dead' and you have thirty quid burning a hole in your pocket then have a look at Ewan the Dream Sheep. Ewan is a soft toy that claims to help your baby settle down to a peaceful sleep by replicating the soothing sounds of a pregnant mother's womb. We just called him 'hypno-sheep'.

Did it work? I don't know. Maybe. Sometimes. To be honest, if it gave us even one decent night's sleep, it was worth every penny. Hypno-sheep was a bit weird though. It emits a low base frequency and pink glow that reminds me of brainwashing scenes in movies. Maybe not as disturbing as A Clockwork Orange, but perhaps a little bit Total Recall or the Manchurian Candidate. I don't know what that bloody sheep is telling my daughter, but if she grows up with a vague memory of living on Mars, or turns into a covert assassin, then I'm having stern words with John Lewis.

The one gadget you simply can't do without is a baby monitor – unless of course you live in a one-room bedsit and are unable to escape your infant's squeaks, snores, farts and whistles. Ours was a pretty basic model which broadcast our child's wailing to a handset, which we carried around the house or as far as the patio. If you live two doors down from a decent pub then you may want to invest in a baby monitor with a decent range.

Really? Of course, I'm kidding although I've heard of a few parents doing this. As you'd imagine, there are a very wide range of monitors to choose from. Some are increasingly sophisticated and feature online video so you can even keep a watchful eye on your sleeping infant whilst you're overseas for work. The problem with these things is that pretty much anyone with a computer can watch your child too. Before you go out and buy such a widget, be mindful of a recent case in Ohio where some creepy hacker gained control of a family's wireless baby monitor and watched the child's shocked reaction when he shouted "wake up baby!" through the intercom.

Sophie the Giraffe doesn't come with optional Wi-Fi. For the uninitiated, Sophie is a chewable rubber toy in the shape of a tiny giraffe that babies love to gnaw on and drool over, like a lion might in a David Attenborough documentary - but mercifully without the giraffe's blood and guts pouring over your beige shag pile carpet.

Sophie is the ultimate baby chew toy. She's been around since 1961 and sold more than fifty million units. I bet you're thinking, gosh, that's probably more than the actual population of giraffes on the entire planet. And you'd be right - the Giraffe Conservation Foundation currently estimates there are around eighty thousand giraffes left. That's a sobering thought, but you can hardly blame fifty million teething babies for the lack of lanky, even-toed ungulated mammals in the African savanah. Sophie the giraffe actually has more in common with a typical dog's toy. Both are chewable, made of rubber and squeak, but I'm sure you don't pay nearly twenty quid for something you'd give your labradoodle to drool over and destroy.

I've never attempted a bungee jump, despite once living in New Zealand for six months (but that's another story). That didn't stop me putting my first born into a baby door bouncer, which is essentially a bungee jump for babies. By all accounts they're safe and my first born happily sprung about in one as he discovered what his legs were for. Still, I kept thinking it looked like a horrible accident masquerading as a comedy YouTube video waiting to happen.

I couldn't get past the uneasy expectation he'd either spring high enough into the air he'd hit the doorframe, or the fixtures would unravel and clobber him. When my daughter grew big enough, we replaced the bungee contraption with something called a jumperoo, which is basically a sprung chair harness with an orchestra of overenthusiastic boogie-woogie music and braying zebra noises.

She was safe enough (unless she discovered some secret emergency ejector button) and happily distracted long enough I could put the kettle on.

My only issue was the volume. In fairness, most children's toys are annoyingly loud and spend their meagre battery life going 'SPROING, YIPPEE! NEIGH! WHOOP WHOOP! MARY HAD A LITTLE LAMB' whilst your sanity slowly and quietly leaves the building.

Let me share a great tip with you - sellotape. Find the speaker and wrap it in sticky tape, it will dampen the volume by at least fifty per cent. It's much better than walking around your home with ear mufflers attached to your head.

The activity mat is less of a toy and more like a mini one square metre bedsit for babies (I looked it up, this tiny space would cost more than £5,000 in most London boroughs).

Before your baby is mobile, she'll either be carried around in your arms or spend her day lying on her mat. They'e all quite similar really although some have been partly inspired by those stuffed tiger rugs once all the rage in Victorian high society, so your child appears to be rolling about on the stomach of some bemused elephant or cross-eyed panda.

She will happily while away the hours lying on her back, trying to reach the bumblebees, unicorns, monkeys and stars dangling just out of her reach. There are always a lot of hoops too, like the monkey bars at the playground. Their task appears to be to inspire your little one to become a trapeze artist. The only baby who might have a hope of such a feat is Maggie from The Simpsons, Maggie could use her activity map to backflip out of her confinement like a champion gymnast, but what you must remember about Maggie Simpson is (a) she has been one year old for 26 years, which makes her 27 now, and (b) let's not forget she is only a fictional character and NOT REAL

Thanks to the internet, there is an almost limitless range of baby tat to choose from. You can get dummies (pacifiers) with a plastic moustache, so your baby looks like a character from a PG Wodehouse book. There are suction devices for decongesting the snot from your beloved. There's a harness called 'Mr Milker' where you can strap on a pair of milk bottles and pretend to be mummy (sounds a bit kinky to me). The Zaky is a highly disturbing pair of artificial hands that you can fit around your baby and fool them into thinking you are holding them, when you are in fact picking your nose and channel surfing. And did you ever wish you could put your child in a straight-jacket to stop them poking about in their filthy nappy? Well, now you can. It's called the 'Baby Budaboo'.

There are also a range of apps for your phone designed to inform, entertain and bemuse. You can try soothing them to sleep with 'White Noise Baby' which will mimic a vacuum cleaner, on an endless loop. I know, it sounds like hell, doesn't it? Wayne Rooney apparently can't sleep without listening to a vacuum cleaner so perhaps he'd like it. Other apps can help you log and record how often your baby is feeding, which may be useful with new-borns in particular. My wife found this helpful with our first child because we wanted to be sure he was getting enough to eat. As is often the way, when we had our second baby we just shrugged and thought, well, she looks alright to me.

If you want, there are apps that will ask for your infant's birthdate and proceed to bombard you with regular updates on your kid's development. All of which you might find helpful, especially if you are a first-time parent, but don't forget every baby will develop at their own pace. If you find you are shouting at your phone saying 'BUT SHE'S NOT WALKING YET' then just delete the app and have a glass of wine (no, not at breakfast).

Sticky fingers

A re-run of Great British Bake Off is showing on the 'People Baking Cakes in the Shape of Elephants whilst Eating Huge Cheeseburgers' channel. It reminds me that before I started this full-time looking after baby malarkey, I'd harboured the stunningly ambitious and quickly abandoned intention to do more baking. After all, I'd have all this time, right? Wrong, wrong, wrong. Some days are considered an achievement if I can do the laundry AND open a tin of beans for lunch. The prospect of setting aside an hour or so to make something that we can't even eat for dinner, quickly seemed utterly ludicrous.

I daydreamed for a moment that I was in the Bake Off tent. Mel and Sue asked for a biographical three-tiered cake that represents my life to date. There I am, balancing the needs of my screaming infant whilst tempering chocolate, before

Daddy Top Tip
There are two types of bibs - the plastic ones with a curved pocket to catch your infant's food, or the cloth variety that offer virtually full-body protection. If the meal is dry and chunky, go with the plastic sort. If the meal is wet and messy, go with the washable full body protection. In extreme cases (spaghetti bolognese, for instance) don't be afraid to use both.

offering my gateau to Mary and Paul. Mary acknowledges I did "pretty jolly well" considering I had a baby to take care of, although the result is "a little informal". Paul, meanwhile, rudely pokes the cake with his index finger and says "It tastes like shit - did you wash your hands after you changed that nappy?"

I'll admit, I'm not a great cook. I can follow a recipe but that's about it. If you are planning to share several months parental leave then like me, you are likely to be looking after your baby from about the age of six months. This is weaning time, the point in your child's development when you need to begin supplementing their diet of milk with real food.

This is important. A good diet helps your child develop and grow, it gives them energy, helps them sleep and boosts their immune system. No pressure then, eh?

There are two approaches to weaning your baby. Either you puree their food and spoon it into them - and your child will grab the spoon and insert in their ear or nose, or knock it away and cover you in puree. Or you offer them

small pieces of whole food which they can learn to feed themselves - which will see ninety per cent of their meal squashed between their little fingers and stuffed down the side of their highchair. Or you can spread your bet and try a combination of both puree and finger food for maximum carnage.

You may encounter parents with quite extreme opinions when it comes to feeding. This can be particularly common with first-time parents. It's natural enough and I'm pretty sure we were more strict with our son's diet than we were second time around with Squeaky. If you see pots of carrot batons at a four-year old's birthday party then it's a good indicator it's the parents first child. By the time you get around to the second child you know no-one is going to eat the carrots and that an afternoon of pizza and cheesy wotsits isn't going to harm them.

Take the finger food vs spooning debate. Some mums (and dads too) will view finger food as a recipe for a choking disaster, others will never offer their child puree because it's restricting the development of their little one's hand-eye co-ordination. Some will never offer their infants any meat, others view the microwave like it's a dying nuclear reactor.

Daddy Top Tip
You will need a highchair - it doesn't need to be fancy or pretty - it needs to be practical. You will be cleaning enough Weetabix fragments and squashed raisins from your highchair's nooks and crevices that you could start your own, albeit unappetising, range of muesli. Get a chair with easy to wipe, smooth rounded edges - I have always liked the cheap Ikea model.

We had a neighbour who was a militant vegetarian and told us off for offering the kids Fruit Shoots at our own son's birthday. Like everything in parenting, do what you think is right, follow your instincts - and if another parent sounds like they're Mussolini in the kitchen, then bite your tongue and do your best to politely ignore them.

The Grapes of Wrath

Daddy Top Tip
Grapes might look innocent enough - but be careful, they are potentially the Dexter of soft fruit (like the forensic technician in the TV series

Grrr!

they are prone to casual murder but you'd never suspect them). Personally, I've always been a little suspicious of the green ones - sour little buggers - but I digress, you must never offer your infant a whole grape. They are the perfect size for blocking your child's throat. The solution is simple enough - slice them in half, vertically from top to bottom and they will be disarmed and ready for the snack box.

Idiots guide to finger food

- Carbs: cooked pasta shapes (penne and fusilli are easy for small hands, spaghetti is a freaking nightmare)
- Dairy: small sticks of cheese (cheddar and babybel are good, but no sweaty stilton and miss the fondue – it's a health and safety catastrophe at the best of times)
- Fruit and veg: soft fruit, such as peaches, pears and strawberries are perfect, firmer fruit such as apples may need a few minutes to steam and soften. Carrots and cucumbers chop nicely into handy sticks
- Eggs were always a quick and versatile meal for Squeaky – even this idiot can bang out an omelette in a minute or two. Don't forget to check for egg allergies by giving them a small taste first.
- Finger food is safe but you must supervise and keep an eye on them
- Make sure pieces of food aren't too big to prevent a choking hazard
- Don't immediately offer them plates or cutlery - they will only become dangerous projectile weapons

Idiots guide to spooning

- Puréed vegetables: carrot, butternut squash, courgette and parsnips are sweet and easy to cook and mash
- Puréed fruit: bananas, apples, pears and avocado (preferably ripe fruit)
- Baby macaroni pieces in sauce, or any pasta that you have cooked and pureed
- Yoghurt is always popular (Squeaky is obsessed with yoghurt – plain and flavoured - I haven't found a flavour she won't eat yet but then I haven't offered her blackcurrant and liquorice – what do you think I am? A sadist?)
- Avoid baby porridge - it's colourful cardboard box has more nutritional value than its processed contents (use regular porridge)

Food allergies appear to be on the rise, so if your family has a history of food allergies, treat the following with caution and carefully monitor: eggs, nuts, kiwi fruit and soy products.

Ready made jars and pouches of baby food are a great standby and it's worth having a variety in your store cupboard. Even if you can ace it in the kitchen like a super daddy, there will be times when you just can't be bothered, or you're going out and need something easily transportable with you. The days when baby food looked and smelled a bit like cat food are thankfully gone and there's now a wide choice, ranging from roast beef to Thai chicken.

Recipes

If you are reading this now and you're still at a complete loss at what to cook for dinner tonight, then buy a chicken. Take it out the fridge for half hour so it's room temperature, drizzle some oil over it, a few herbs, shove a lemon up its arse and whack it in the oven at 180 degrees for an hour. No one will go hungry.

The other cast-iron fail-safe option in our house is a good spaghetti bolognese. It's great because the whole family will enjoy it, it's easy to freeze and re-heat for batch cooking, plus it's terrific for blending and hiding some veg (for those fussier eaters).

I was particularly proud of some baby soufflés I made from a River Cottage recipe book - basically some whisked egg mixture, with some chicken and spinach filling that you bake in a muffin tray. They rose beautifully in the oven and I felt great pride unveiling these perfectly risen, little golden morsels of goodness. After they'd cooled, I offered one to my daughter.

"Here you go, darling - it's super yummy" I told her.

She took one disinterested look at my culinary achievement, before crumbling my lovingly crafted meal in her hand and air-dropping it on the floor.

Sigh. She's like one of those food critics on MasterChef. I fully expect her first words will be "Daddy, it lacks seasoning".

She's on the move

Some of the most joyous experiences as a parent are the moments your baby first rolls over, crawls for the first time and when they take their first tentative steps. There is a unique joy in watching your helpless infant achieve these stages in their development. It will fill your heart with love and pride, bring a tear to your eye and on a practical level, will prove to be an absolute bloody nightmare.

Gone are the days when you'd be able to lie your baby on the floor, nip to the toilet and be reasonably confident they'll still be where you left them. Sure, she'd flop her arms about, kick her legs and approximate the behaviour of a beached dolphin, but she wasn't going anywhere.

Now she's on the move - anything is possible. You might think, well, she can only roll over - how far can she go? How about that six inch gap beneath the sofa, where the stray toys and old phone charger cables live? Yep, in less time than it takes to boil a kettle, she'll be in like Flynn and covered from head to toe in dirt and wrapped up in your old Nokia cable.

Have you ever seen army manoeuvres, where they roll repeatedly like an errant kitchen towel, to avoid enemy gunfire? That's your baby now. So, if you think you can take a shower, make a cup of tea or go for a number two, without the constant fear of your child rolling out the door, then think again.

You might need to think about baby proofing your home – look out for coffee tables which she might easily flip over, remove anything made of glass with sharp edges and corners. It sounds hard but it's amazing what can be achieved with a roll of cellophane, some sticky tape and an empty egg carton. Still, I'm surprised no-one had invented an oversized plastic hamster ball big enough to roll an enthusiastic toddler around your home in.

Try laying down some ground rules. "You can crawl wherever you like and play with whatever you want – but no going into the kitche , no climbing up the stairs, do not use my Neil Young LP as a chew toy and no drinking from daddy's booze trolley."

Actually, keep it to one instruction at a time. She's more likely to listen and understand. The downside is that whilst you may have prevented her from scooting into the kitchen to practice knife juggling, I'm afraid she's still rolling bottles of vodka across the floor and eating your copy of After the Gold Rush.

What else can you do? Well, it's generally considered bad form these days to use a playpen - a little baby cage, which your lovable little blighter is unable to escape from. Baby bouncers can be a lifesaver in these situations, until your infant outgrows it. Of course, they're not the only socially acceptable way of tieing your child to a chair. Do you think that sounds mean? Who on earth would tie their baby to a chair? Well, what on earth do you think the straps on a highchair are for?

Incidentally, if you think your baby is safely strapped into their highchair and there's no way she is going anywhere, then I will tell you 'Do not underestimate your child'. They're all little escapologists. One time, I took my eye off Squeaky long enough to sort the laundry - I was in the next room, the door wide open - and yet within two short minutes, she'd pulled herself upright and was planking so hard her straps barely contained her from free-falling to the floor.

It's always worth trying to reason with your baby – they understand and wilfully ignore more than you'd suppose. "I'm gonna put some toast on darling, could you please try not to headplant the floor for thirty seconds?" And maybe she will, or maybe she won't, but you will spend every moment waiting for a noise like a Harrier Jump Jet crashing through Arnold Schwarzanegger's front room.

David
Bowie vs
the Mr Men

It's hard to say this without cackling like Sid James in a Carry On film, but I've nothing against a bit of humpty dumpty. Or perhaps you prefer a rousing rendition of hickory dickory dock? But as much as I love a good nursery rhyme, your baby's just as likely to enjoy Coldplay or Beyonce. Sure, wind the bobbin up has hand movements, but it's really just as easy to teach your little one to clap along to Marc Bolan's 'Bang a Gong (Get it On)'. In time, your children will dictate what music you listen to, so get the ground work in early and brain wash/share your love of music with them as soon as possible.

Is this a dad thing? I'm not saying that a mum won't endlessly obsess over the perfect age to introduce her son to Take That. I know one mum who blanket bans the Gummy Bear song in favour of a nutritionally balanced diet of Metallica, but I suspect a dad is more likely to think carefully over whether their baby will prefer The Beatles to The Rolling Stones.

I don't know if you have noticed this, but since becoming a dad I've spotted a somewhat disturbing trend in song lyrics. It doesn't matter what genre you listen to - country, hip hop, rock, pop, metal - if the song isn't about love, or more bluntly sex, then it's about how crap their dad is. Too often, dad is a feckless sleazebag and womaniser (The Temptation's Papa

Was a Rolling Stone) or he had the audacity to prematurely pop his clogs (The Who's Tommy and Pink Floyd's The Wall). It's the same story in hip hop. Tupac Shakur raged at his dad for forcing him to "play catch by himself" whilst his mum entertained men to pay the rent.

That said, I've some sympathy for the dad in Madonna's Papa Don't Preach (yeah, you can keep your baby but why the hell didn't you use a condom?) Seriously, you could fill an entire book with music's crap dads: Jane's Addiction's Had a Dad, The Beach Boy's I'm Bugged At My Ol Man, Genesis' No Son of Mine. My favourite has to be Jonny Cash's A Boy Named Sue where the son is understandably pissed at his dad for giving him a girl's name.

For the sake of balance, try to think of a song that has something positive to sing about dad. No? Me neither, well there's Daddy Cool by Boney M but that's about your lot.

One of my little daddy rituals was classic album hour with the kids. We'd listen to quite a range of music until I put on my old childhood favourite, a Mr Men LP. It's actually a pretty terrific album, evocative of the folky experimentalism of the 1970s.

The problem was, for several months, every time I tried to put a different record on, my son asked for the Mr Men.

What you playing?

Paul Simon

I want Mr Men

What are you playing?

Muppet Show

Muppet Show?

I love Mu....
You love The Muppet Show?
I want Mr Men

And y'know I've learned that his obsession with the Mr Men is a wonderful, healthy, natural thing. Looking at the state of the record sleeve, I suspect I was similarly possessed by Mr Tickle and Mr Greedy when I was his age. And in truth, you can wave your arms and pogo like a crazy thing to the Mr Men, which is more than you can say for Bob Dylan.

The other great thing about being a stay at home dad is that babies love embarrassing dad stuff. Your days of clubbing and gigging might be all but over, but you now have a great opportunity to embrace your inner air guitar and unleash your most enthusiastic dad dancing.

An exuberant air trumpet solo is not only great fun, but it's a useful way of averting a toddler meltdown. She's screaming over her toast? Sing Bowie's Heroes. She's howling over

MR DAVID BOWIE

dropping Mr Bear? Put on some Daft Punk and wave your hands in the air, like you just don't care. Your baby might machine gun her peas all over the floor like a well oiled Uzi, but she won't discriminate against your taste in music. Not yet anyway.

My six months at home with my daughter happened to coincide with the untimely departure of David Bowie. Over the following weeks, I played everything from Life on Mars to Let's Dance. 'Changes' became the soundtrack to cleaning her bum:

Ch-ch-ch-changes
Turn and face the strain
Ch-ch-ch-changes...

And then, a few months after the shock of Bowie dying, we lost Prince. I held Squeaky in my arms and danced around the house to Raspberry Beret, with a tear in my eye and a smile on my face as my daughter giggled happily. I took to dressing her in purple, just so that I could sing:

I never meant to cause you any sorrow

I never meant to cause you any pain

I only want to see you

In your purple socks

Purple socks, purple socks...

I didn't see any harm in it, but perhaps I shouldn't have waved a banana under her nose to Prince's 'Sexy Mother Fucker'. Bad daddy? I don't know. The jury's still out.

Jobs around the house

Y ou might be thinking, I'm home with the baby for a few months, I can finally catch up on those jobs around the house. I thought that too and I can tell you after six months at home with my daughter, the flush handle on the toilet still needs replacing, the bathroom tap still drips and the power is still out in the shed. So, if you are thinking of redecorating the backroom whilst looking after your progeny, then good luck to you, you poor deluded fool.

It might, just might be possible to complete some small tasks around the house but you need to manage your expectations of what is possible. One afternoon, whilst my wife was at work and both children appeared happily distracted by the Brio train set, I quickly went to the shed, mixed some Poylfilla in an old bowl and fixed a small hole in the wall of the downstairs hall that had eluded me for almost three years.

I can tell you, the immense pride and satisfaction I felt, anyone would think I'd knocked up a two-bedroom extension. But doing anything, anything at all, even going for a piss is like climbing Everest when there's two little people demanding every moment of your attention.

Where I'd patched the wall was a bit rough though. Then I remembered my dad advising using a damp cloth to get a smooth finish. What I needed was a wet wipe so I crept past the kids so as not to disturb their play, grabbed the change bag and achieved a lovely finish with a single disposable wet wipe. That got me to thinking, what else could be achieved with the contents of a nappy bag?

1. Nappies make a great temporary fix for a leaking pipe before the plumber arrives

2. Catch oil spills using a nappy when changing the oil in your car

3. Oven gloves in the wash? Just slip on a couple of nappies

4. You can pack and protect fragile items using nappies

5. Wet wipes are very effective for removing matt paint from your hands when you're decorating

6. Fire proof your belongings. Disposable nappies contain something called sodium polyacrylate. It's what they make flame retardant gels from. In the event of an impending wildfire, why not fire proof your stuff by wrapping them with a wet nappy? I'll admit, this may be more relevant if you're sat in Colorado and less helpful if you're in Putney

7. Wet wipes are terrific at catching those little spills, but let's face it, they're less than adequate when your child tips their entire breakfast all over the floor. Instead of using half a packet of wet wipes, man up and grab a nappy - they're super absorbent (as those adverts repeatedly tell us). One quick wipe with a damp nappy and 'hey presto', you have a clean floor!

8. It's Christmas and you're in charge of envelope licking. To prevent the taste of glue in your mouth, use a trusty wet wipe to dab the envelopes instead

Go to sleep!

Sleep! Go to sleep! Why won't you sleep? Please, for the love of God, just stop crying and go to sleep. SLEEP!!!!!

Repeat these words in your head like a mantra, as if you can somehow telepathically use your will to sedate your child. It's worth a try, but needless to say, it never works. A lack of sleep may well be the greatest challenge you will face. All of the mess and screaming, chores and chaos can be handled if you had a decent night's rest. Equally, every challenge of parenthood can seem virtually impossible if you are being awoken constantly in the night and your child refuses to nap.

You should already be familiar with a certain amount of sleep deprivation, but in all likelihood your partner probably took the brunt of the sleepless nights so you could survive going to work. As the roles switch and you become the full-time carer, it's only fair that you take on more of the night-shift. Maybe you're thinking, but that means I'm on duty 24 hours a day? Yep. I said it was fair. I never said it would be fun.

Sleep deprivation is a commonly used interrogation technique and in less tolerant societies, an instrument of torture. You quickly reach a point where you are operating on some mechanical level. Your body seems to know it's changing a nappy or mixing a bottle but you are only dimly aware of your actions. You start dropping things and walking into large inanimate objects like closed doors. It can even affect your speech. When you apologise to the woman in the Co-op and explain that you're "sleep depraved", you'll have no idea why the security man rugby tackled you into the cold meats section. If you're lucky, there will be a quiet voice in your head (as they drag you off) saying 'I meant sleep deprived, I'm far too tired to be depraved!'

Your thoughts become sort of slippery and a bit fudged together. At least, mine did. It was an odd time. I was looking after Squeaky in the first half of 2016, which may be remembered by future generations as the year of the terrible apocalypse of talent which started promptly with the death of Bowie in January.

The news stream of obituaries was relentless and blended in my mind with the latest developments in Game of Thrones. Would Terry Wogan, Gene Wilder, Muhammed Ali and Ronnie Corbett become white-walkers and invade Westeros? It was a disturbing image, reinforced by the fact that the recently departed David Gest, with his face like a melted panini, had resembled the undead for some years already.

This book does not have all the answers to ensuring your child sleeps well. I'm not sure it has any answers, to be honest. Most parenting books obsess over sleeping techniques - let them cry or don't let them cry, let them sleep with you or don't let them sleep with you. All I will say is that sharing a bed with two women was not at all how I imagined and largely involved being repeatedly kicked in the face by little feet.

I said I didn't have any answers, but every parent has a technique for getting their babies off to sleep. I'll share mine with you - it's called the Indiana Jones.

I often find myself standing over my daughter's cot, holding her in my arms as she falls asleep. Getting a baby to sleep is no easy thing, but harder still is getting her to sleep and putting her down without waking her up.

It might be the most singularly exhausting and patience depleting endeavour you experience as a parent, or one of them at least. And Indy would be crap at it. Why?

Cast your mind back to Raiders of the Lost Ark. Indy is standing in front of the little golden idol, with a bag of sand at the ready. He trickles a little out and then quickly lifts the prize whilst dropping the bag of sand in its place.

That's what is in my mind every time I managed to rock my daughter to sleep before carefully placing her in her cot. If I am successful, she will stay asleep and I can retreat successfully and have a well deserved cup of tea. If I fail, a high pitched wail fills the air as I run down the stairs, two at a time, pursued by a large rolling boulder as spears projectile from the wallpaper. You see, Indy failed the test. I'm sure if he were in my shoes, he'd be racing from a crying baby, fedora grasped over his ears to dampen the noise. So, how can you pass the Indy test?

First, your baby must be tired. Warning signs include a stifled yawn, a glazed expression or increased crankiness or a particular need to be held. What do you mean? They always want to be held? He's always cranky? You'll learn your infant's signs, after all you will go through this ritual three times a day.

People always talk about rocking a baby to sleep, implying a left to right motion, but I always found a gentle up and down movement more successful. Lift your heels off the ground or bend your knees. I like to imagine I'm a policeman in a black and white movie. Just resist the temptation to say "Ello, ello, what have we got here then?"

Once they are asleep in your arms, congratulate yourself (quietly) but now it is time for the tricky bit. How do you get her down without waking her? Well, you are going to need to be patient. You're gonna need to out-Buddha the Dalai Llama. Start by counting to a hundred. If you're like me, you'll get bored, drift off and not make it past 37.

So, think of something else, hum some music in your head, do a quick mental inventory of the jobs you want to catch up on and the most efficient use of your time once you have successfully extricated yourself from your beloved infant. If it's morning nap time you may only have 30 minutes, so for the sake of your sanity, put the kettle on, before you do anything else.

A couple minutes have now passed since she fell asleep, she's still in your arms. Have one last attempt at counting to 100, if you didn't make it last time, you certainly won't this time but the longer you hold on before putting her down, the better your chances you won't wake her up.

Time for a controlled landing. Gently remove her from your chest and lower her to her cot. Don't rush, you don't want to fumble this. As you place her onto the mattress, keep one hand beneath her and use the other to pat her tummy. You need to maintain body contact. You may need to keep this going for a couple of minutes, then slowly release your hand from beneath her, whilst maintaining the patting.

Then, finally, slow the patting before withdrawing your hand, tip-toe across the nursery and hope to Christ the floorboards don't squeak. In your face, Indy, you won - who's the daddy? You are, my friend. Now drink that tea before she wakes up. Oh, go on, have a biscuit, you earned it.

I found it was taking me half-an-hour to get my daughter off for her morning and afternoon naps - and when she finally went to sleep, she'd wake up after twenty minutes. It was very frustrating. Instead, I'd bundle her up in the pushchair, regardless of the weather and march around the block until she nodded off. The pushchair has a number of advantages. Even if she takes awhile to nod off, in the meantime you're getting some fresh air and exercise.

You may even be able to combine it with a trip to the Co-op or some other errand. When she does fall asleep, you don't have to worry about moving her - you just park her up in the hall and let her sleep in the pushchair. There is an art to this though. I found that I needed to maintain a steady pace to help her relax to sleep. It was like a cheap remake of the Keanu Reeves film, Speed. If the pushchair dropped below three miles per hour she'd explode.

You may also want to think about your route. Say, for arguments sake, it typically takes fifteen minutes steady walking to get her off to the land of nod. If you walk fifteen minutes away from home, before she's asleep, then walk the fifteen minutes home, you may only have a few short minutes before she wakes up. Barely enough time to make a cup of tea. To maximise your time whilst your baby is napping, work out a circular route from your home that gets you home a few minutes after she falls asleep. That should give you at least half-an-hour to hang the laundry, prepare a meal, gulp back a cup of coffee before she wakes up demanding your full and undivided attention.

Little
fish

It's a great idea to get your child into a swimming pool as soon as possible - it can build confidence that sets them up for years to come. But I was a little worried when an email arrived from the swim school. They explained, matter of factly, that the changing room would be mixed and there would be a 'temporary partition' to separate the mums from the dads. It sounded more than a little flimsy and 'temporary' gave the impression that someone was waiting for the opportune moment to pull the partition down and scream "I CAN SEE THAT MAN'S DING DONG!"

Swimming with a baby requires an optimum level of organisation on your part. Like some oversized boy scout without the woggle (whatever happened to woggles?) you need to be prepared - very prepared. You must remember swimming costumes (yours and hers), towels (yours and hers), swimming nappies (disposable and rubber incontinence pants (hers, not yours - I hope), a clean nappy and change of clothes (hers) and probably a bottle of warm milk on standby and/or snack to placate her whilst you get changed.

What you really don't want to do is find yourself hopping about in the changing rooms naked as the day you were born, with a screaming infant whilst attempting to dry off with six inches of muslin cloth because you forgot the towels. Me? Would I do that? Uh. You might think that, but I couldn't possibly comment...

Trust me, getting changed at a swimming pool with a baby is no picnic, especially when you have both just got out the pool. Her body temperature is plumetting, you are both cold and wet and any surface you can find to put her down on is hard as concrete.

It doesn't help when you find yourself in a changing room the size of a small bathroom with twelve mums and dads trying to get six babies dressed - and there's only three cubicles, with a plastic shower curtain for modesty.

My mistake, make that potentially twenty-four mums and dads getting a dozen babies changed because you always have an outgoing and incoming class. But there are still only three cubicles.

This is the situation my sister, Eve, and her husband, Andy, found themselves in. Amidst the chaos of frantic sleep-deprived parents and screaming babies, my sister was changing her daughter by the side of the pool. Meanwhile, my brother-in-law was getting changed in a cubicle when a mum swiped open the curtain as he was in a state of complete undress. He was able to joke about the experience afterwards, but it was all really rather embarassing.

It's fair to say swimming classes struggle a bit with accomodating dads. Is it worth the trouble? The good news is that taking your baby swimming is an utter delight. There you are with a small child who can't walk, crawl or even roll over - then you put them in the water and they're happily splashing about. You can call them 'little fish' but for me, the experience brings to mind the penguin pool at London Zoo where these awkward creatures stumble about on land and transform unexpectedly into such graceful swimmers when they hit the water. Although, nobody has thrown a bucket of fish and krill at us yet.

Baby swimming classes are surprisingly full on. Within moments of getting into the water, Squeaky was fully submerged without so much as a winge. I'd fully expected her to kick off with a 'WHAT THE HELL ARE YOU DOING,

DADDY?' scream, but she was entirely nonplussed. I expected armbands. No armbands. And nobody sunk their baby. Not even once. Sure, you hold onto them, but even then, it's not long before the instructor is telling you to give them a shove and let them go. You don't feel scared because you assume these people have succeeded in running this business without losing any babies, but it's still pretty crazy stuff, letting a seven-month-old baby loose in five feet of water. And of course, there are seven or eight other parents with babies doing what you are doing, so not only does it feel safe, but you look like some cross generational synchronized swimming routine.

Plus, it's a great opportunity to completely focus on your child in the here and now. Sure, there might be some honey in a bikini but she can't compete with the smile your daughter gave you when you surfed her through the water as you hummed the theme tune to Hawaii Five-0.

Maybe next week, we'll try a double reverse pike off the diving board.

Pottery
and raves

W e've already mentioned playgroups and swim classes, but the baby industry now offers you a bewildering selection of activities to take your infant along to.

Some are more naturally dad friendly than others. I wouldn't suggest going along to a post-natal yoga class, for instance. These classes are particularly aimed at convalescing mums after a difficult childbirth and they're unlikely to appreciate you being there whilst their downward facing dog looks like it needs a vet. Besides, I'm reliably informed by my wife that post-natal yoga classes are less about relaxing and more about stopping your baby stealing some other kids socks and mucking up another mum's karma.

I used to take Padawan along to Monkey Music when he was little. He'd sit on my lap and we'd be in a circle singing songs and banging maracas against a drum. It was fun as these things go, but expensive – you had to block book the classes by the term, so if you were sick or on holiday, you still had to pay. I think we got as much fun out of the nursery rhyme sing song at our local church playgroup and that was a fraction of the price AND you get a cup of tea and a biscuit.

Pottery cafes are becoming increasingly popular. You'll need to book ahead though because they're usually packed with mums creating some bespoke artwork with their infant's handprint. I was dangerously ambitious one half-term and took both kids along to create something memorable for my wife's pending birthday. It was bloody stressful, I'll be honest. My son had his eye on giving a £30 stegosaurus a damn good Jackson Pollocking and Squeaky refused to sit still. I was moments from abandoning ship and making for the nearest exit when an assistant mercifully arrived, clutching handfuls of paints and coasters. Within minutes we'd created personalised presents for not only my wife but also scored brownie points with both sets of grandparents. All for less than the price of a dinosaur dipped in several shades of purple.

I'm not sure I should be here!

Baby massage is a great bonding experience with your infant and it can even help your baby's digestive system and relax them so they sleep more easily. No, I can't promise it will work, but it's got to be worth a try. I sat in a circle of mums (I was the only dad, as usual) as a small bottle of olive oil was passed around. We'd then pour the oil onto our hands and massage our children's tummy, shoulders, arms and legs. It's pretty much the same as marinating a chicken but you don't put a lemon up their bum afterwards. Or use seasoning.

I may have mentioned that you can't go clubbing now you have a baby, but that's not strictly true. A handful of enterprising clubs have opened their doors during daylight hours and turned the volume down. Parents can take their little ones for a rave and possibly reminisce about the time they sneezed their best mate's cocaine onto the toilet floor. Oh, how times have changed. Now, the white powder is milk formula and you don't recognise any of the music. You can still wave a glow stick in the air like you just don't care, but now you have to change your dance partner's nappy.

If none of these take your fancy, you can always take your baby to learn how to Charleston, discover baby ballet, explore gymnastics, baking for tots or teach them to be the next Beckham. Although, you may need to wait until they can walk first.

Eating out

There are a whole bunch of things you are no longer able to easily do now that you have a small infant. You can't pop out for a quiet pint, visit the gym, get your haircut, stay out all night or go see a show. What's left, you might well ask?

You can eat out. Most restaurants are family friendly. After all, three or four hungry mouths spend more money than two, especially since small children tend to put away a surprisingly large quantity of food. My wife likes to say that our daughter can eat more meals than Frodo. That's quite impressive because the hobbits from The Lord of the Rings can put away breakfast, second breakfast, elevenses, lunch, afternoon tea and dinner before finishing the day with supper.

The key to enjoying a meal out with a small child is to choose the right establishment and be prepared. I wouldn't go booking the seven-course taster menu and taking your baby with you, although we have done just that. My overriding memory of lunch at the two-Michelin star restaurant L'Enclume is of me marching around Cartmel with the pushchair in a desperate effort to subdue my screaming child whilst my infusion of smoked pheasant with foraged herbs turned to slop.

Perhaps we were slightly optimistic but your options do extend beyond McDonalds. Actually, I found the staff at our local Maccy D to be incredibly helpful and would insist on carrying my tray of food whilst I navigated the pushchair with a highchair balanced on my head.

We didn't go very often, but if I was in town and Squeaky had an urgent attack of the munchies, I knew I could have chicken nuggets and a selection of fresh fruit in front of her in less time than it takes to catch a waitresses eye.

Nandos was a different matter. Despite the appearance of being a "proper restaurant" the waiter insisted on showing me to a table and then insisted I go back to the counter to place my order, which required picking up Squeaky and carrying her around the restaurant when I was attempting to settle her.

Perhaps our most stressful eating experience was a ramen noodle bar called Bone Daddies, which was crowded with hipsters perched on high stools, listening to Guns'n'Roses. The lack of space made life difficult with a baby and a four year old, but the absence of chairs accompanied with big bowls of scorching hot broth proved to be the stuff of nightmares.

The lesson here is choose your establishment wisely – some place with highchairs, where they're likely to tolerate some (or a lot of) noise and mess and there's enough space to make an emergency escape if they throw a sustained tantrum.

In a lot of respects you have a wider choice of eateries when your baby is younger than six-months. I took Amy to the fancy Vanilla Pod in Marlow a couple of times for the set lunch and Squeaky would quietly snooze through the mushroom risotto, fillet of beef and chocolate mousse. Well, apart from the time she woke up screaming, having shat herself senseless and I had to commandeer the upstairs hall to mop her up. I still can't eat chocolate mousse without suffering horrific flashbacks.

When Squeaky reached six months, we'd put her in a highchair and let her feed herself with a little of whatever we were eating. It's called a bandit plate. We'd ask for an extra plate and cut a little off our own meals and put it on hers. The upside is that your child gets to experience a wider range of food at a young age and eat something other than burger/sausage/pizza and chips, which is pretty much what every restaurant offers everyone under the age of eighteen. The downside is it's as if the taxman has come along and taken twenty per cent of your meal away. Look at it this way though, you now have the perfect excuse to order a guilt-free pudding because you're still hungry.

You will need to manage your expectations. Little people can't sit still for long so make sure you're somewhere with enough space you can pick them up and walk about for a few minutes. It's also useful to take a bag of small toys to distract them with. Our 'pub bag' has a few finger puppets, action figures, box of raisins, rice crackers, a colouring-in book and some crayons and it's saved our sanity a number of times.

If all that fails, I have no shame in getting my phone out and putting Peppa Pig on. What do you mean it's a bad habit and they should be learning social skills at the dinner table? Balls to that, I say. If it means you and everyone else within a twenty feet radius is going to enjoy their meal in peace then don't feel guilty about it - just perhaps try not to make a habit of it.

Take care not to let them burn their mouths with hot food, which is easily done with an inpatient child if the restaurant is busy. I like to turn Squeaky's plate into a 'lazy susan'. I push the hot food to the far side of her plate, furthest from her curious little hands and put the cooled food nearest her. When she's finished her cooled food, I just spin the plate 180 degrees because the hot food is now cooled and put some fresh hot food on the far side of her plate, and repeat until she is full or we have ran out of food.

Timing is critically important. If your little one is tired, or you think they might be unwell or teething, then just cancel your reservation. Do you really want to spend your meal pleading with your beloved whilst they scream the place down and fling plastic cutlery at the couple next to you? Don't worry, we've all been there, mums and dads alike, although I can't help but suspect the greater pity is reserved for the desperate dads. "That poor man, struggling with that baby – where's their mum?" Yeah, I can read your expression. What, you never seen a mother with a screaming child before?

Finally, leave a decent tip. The very best case scenario is you left an almighty mess, the worse case is you have annoyed everyone in the building and still left a terrible mess, so don't be cheap.

Teething

Do you remember what it was like when your wisdom teeth came through? It grips hold of your jaw and jabs at your brain like a pissed off Muhammad Ali when George Foreman charged him a hundred bucks for a toasted sandwich maker and it broke after four months.

So, spare a thought for your side-kick. One can only suppose a teething baby is being similarly tormented, so try and be patient when she screams day and night, night and day.

What can you do to help? You may have an aged relative tell you that a nip of whiskey 'never did me any harm' but those days are long gone now. What about a teaspoon of Mrs Winslow's Soothing Syrup or Godfrey's Cordial? Not likely - both brands were discontinued long ago and besides, they contained opium or morphine (an opium derivative).

Unless you're intending to bypass your local pharmacy and source your infant's medicinal requirements from Pablo Escobar, your options are rather limited. You can try smearing some bonjela on her gums. With a bit of luck this may soothe her long enough for her to nod off to sleep.

Teething granules are also available (Ashton and Parsons) but you look like you are trying to blow a gram of cocaine onto your infant's gums. These can be a very effective pain relief, but tricky to get into an angry baby's mouth. You might try administering this white powder via a rolled-up twenty pound note, but I would urge you not to. This isn't the Robert Downey Jr school of parenting.

Your little one's teeth will start to come through at about the same time as weaning and trying solid foods. Sore gums will often affect your child's appetite, but offering them cool food can help. Keep an apple in the fridge and offer them a slice to suck on, or a teething ring.

If that doesn't work, wheel out the big guns and give your child a dose of baby paracetomol.

If you're not sure if she's teething or just in a horrible mood, the symptoms for teething include drooling, irritability, swollen gums, incessant chewing and sucking, difficulty sleeping, turning away food and teeth peaking out from her gums. If your labrador has these symptoms, it's probably rabies and remember it's good practice not to confuse your infant with your dog.

If your child is teething then this means it's time to start cleaning her teeth. The NHS guidance rather underestimates the magnitude of this task by advising 'not all children like having their teeth brushed, so you may have to keep on trying'. Talk about an understatement. Your infant will either refuse to open her mouth so you'll need to crowbar her jaw open, or she will happily open her mouth before clamping down on the toothbrush and proceed to chew it's head off with all the violence of a great white shark auditioning for a reboot of Jaws.

If you do manage to get a toothbrush in her mouth (odds of 2:1) and you can move the toothbrush (odds of 5:1) then you are advised to brush the teeth in small, circular motions (odds of 20:1) and get your child to spit the toothpaste out when you have finished (odds of 100:1). Do you have to do this everyday? Well, twice a day actually. Good luck!

First
aid

It's a hell of a thing, being single-handedly responsible for the life of a small, helpless creature. A few weeks before I left work to take care of my baby girl, I had a sudden overwhelming sense of responsibility.

It hit me like a slap in the face. I was going to be at home with my daughter alone and my wife won't be back for ten hours or more - what if something went wrong?

True, I'd always been consulted by my wife when our daughter seemed unwell and I'd have a say in whether some odd skin mark or bout of incessant screaming (as in more than usual) warranted a trip to the doctor.

This was different though. I'd been promoted from co-pilot and was now flying the plane. True, I didn't have a plane load of passengers depending on me, but was this any less of a responsibility? Deep breath. Calm down. I was hyperventilating slightly, can't you tell?

Looking back, the strange thing is how little time it took for this enormous weight of responsibility to become as normal as brewing a cup of tea, but at the beginning, I must admit, it was overwhelming with a capital 'Oh', as in 'OH MY GOD - WHAT DO I DO?'

It was a similar feeling when our son was born and we left the hospital for the first time. I remember thinking - is that it? There's so much energy and preparation for the birth itself, but next to nothing after they're born. We decided on our birthing plan, having taken our pick from a menu of pain relief options from hypnotherapy to epidurals with a side-order of laughing gas. But after your child is born and they've mopped up the mess and stitched up your wife, the hospital pushes you out the door with little more than a hearty 'good luck' and a carrier bag full of discount coupons.

What would I do, if something went wrong?

What you must remember and I had forgotten, is that you won't break your baby. This is something worth repeating:

DO NOT PANIC! YOU WON'T BREAK YOUR BABY!

Obviously, you can't use this book as your main source of first-aid advice. God forbid. But in most cases, if you are worried about your baby's health - for whatever reason, then ring your doctor or the NHS helpline (if you are in the UK). When it comes to the health of a baby, you are rarely wasting your doctor's time. It's important you learn to trust your instincts as a parent to help you decide when you need to get help. The alternative is spending the rest of your natural life in varying degrees of panic, which is no help to anyone.

My main fear was what to do if my daughter choked on her food, especially when I was about to start her on solids for the first time. If she couldn't breathe, I might not have time to get help. Actually, it turns out babies are remarkably efficient at coughing food up that gets caught in their throat. Still, I wanted to know what to do in a worse case scenario, so I signed up on a paedeatric first aid course.

I went with the St John's Ambulance Service, but there are many organisations running similar events. The course I attended was outstanding and covered everything from identifying sickle cell disease to how to resucitate a choking baby. Why these courses aren't compulsory for every parent, I really cannot imagine. It strikes me as rather curious that folk make a fuss about not every member of nursery staff being trained in first-aid but as parents they haven't done it themselves. I cannot recommend it highly enough. It changed me from a gibbering wreck to a much more confident gibbering parent.

I won't cover everything here, but I will briefly explain what to do with a choking baby because it's a useful thing to know as a stay-at-home dad and had been my number one panic button.

It's simple enough. Sit down and lay them face down along your thigh. Then, supporting the baby's head, give up to five sharp blows between their shoulder blades with the heel of your hand. The advice 'sharp blows' is a little intimadating. It gives the impression you're beating the living shit out of your child. The point is, a gentle tap isn't going to cut it, so be firm, not violent.

The truth is you are unlikely to have to cope with anything more than a bout of the Linda Blairs (the vomiting girl with a swivelling head from The Exorcist) or a cold. Still, in my experience Squeaky would nurture a mild case of the sniffles until it grew into THE COUGH, which sounded like she'd spent her afternoons chain smoking unfiltered Benson & Hedges. It kept her and the rest of the house awake repeatedly for several nights.

What can you do? You can try rubbing their chest with vapour rub. I'm not convinced it helps much, but it will make your house smell like a hotel spa, which is just another cruel reminder of something nice you're unlikely to experience for the forseeable future. If your baby is really cross and won't settle down, then there's your old friend drugs, or in your child's case - baby paracetomol, or Calpol.

Incidentally, do not drink the Calpol. By all means try it, but it tastes like a vile and artificially sweet elixir of boiled down, semi-fermented haribo. You may be surprised to hear there is a cocktail named Calpol (2 oz vodka, 12 oz smirnoff ice, 2 oz red bull) that is also deeply unpleasant, but doesn't actually include any childrens paracetomol. Only sick children drink Calpol, with the notable exception of professional alcoholic and one-time football player, Paul (Gazza) Gascoigne. He became hooked on the pink stuff when he heard (incorrectly) it had 0.00001 per cent alcohol in it and thought if he drank enough, he'd get

wasted without looking like he was drinking 'real booze'. So, unless you want to emulate Gazza and look like an ageing, terrifying and oversized baby with chronic kidney problems, staggering into a police siege with a bucket of fried chicken and a fishing rod like some deranged garden gnome then lay off the Calpol. Have a gin and tonic instead or an Old Fashioned (2oz whiskey, 2 dashes Angostura bitters, 1 teaspoon of sugar, dash of water). I don't want to be the one to tell you this, but your days of a Breakfast Martini (1.5 oz gin, 3/4 oz Cointreau, 3/4 oz lemon juice, 1 tsp orange marmalade) or Sex on the Beach (1 oz Peach Schnapps, 2 oz Orange Juice, 2oz Cranberry Juice) are over for the forseeable future.

Daddy Top Tip
Calpol or other childrens paracetamol, childrens ibuprofen, electronic thermometer (my doctor recommended the sort that you insert in the child's ear), baby syringe (to administer the medicine), bonjela and teething granules, sticky plasters, adhesive tape, bandages, sterile gauze dressings, antiseptic cream/spray, antihistamine cream and calamine lotion. You'll probably not use half of these, but it's good to be prepared.

Poop

You'll be amazed how interested you become in the contents of your progeny's nappy. It's a perfect storm of curiosity, professional interest and revulsion.

Taking turns to change the occasional nappy at home was but an unpleasant appetizer to the wide array of nappy filled mayhem that you will endure as a full-time dad. Not only will you be mopping up and chasing these unpleasant suspects around the floor, but no doubt you will be asked to describe how she is pooing to your other half and your new social circle of latte swilling poop obsessed mothers, so to help you, here is a short list of baby poo descriptions in order of size and severity:

Is it a raisin?

Brown grape

Peanut butter

Poo glue

Exploding weetabix

Bum nuggets

Rogan josh

Buried treasure

Fast and the Furious

Poonami

Your nemesis is the poonami, Moriarty to your Sherlock Holmes, Blofeld to your James Bond, but much more dangerous. Measuring 7.5 on the Richter Scale of small infant turds, I can assure you, this tsunami of faecal matter will explode with enough violence to incapacitate any nappy. It will devour and consume your loved one's clothing in a tidal wave of diarrhoea and if you are particulary unlucky render your sofa into such a stinking state that you'll stand there, in a state of shock seriously wondering if you can get away with dragging it into the garden, dousing it in petrol and burning it, perhaps throwing yourself into the burning pyre in a diabolical domestic re-enactment of The Wicker Man, whereupon you realise this will require a trip to Ikea.

If you thought a poonami was the worst you can expect, you'd be sadly mistaken. The public poonami can be exponentially worse. Before I go any further, I'd like to take this opportunity to offer my sincerest and most abject apologies to the Odeon cinema in Aylesbury and in particular anyone who used their disabled toilet on 23 April 2016.

My sister and I had taken our respective babies to the newbies screening of Florence Foster Jenkins, a slightly amusing film about a woman who believes she can perform opera, but in fact has a voice like a bag of angry cats being thrown into Battersea Dogs Home. During the screening, Meryl Streep's singing triggered widespread wailing amongst the little people in the audience and, in response, my daughter dropped a brown bomb in her nappy.

Daddy Top Tip
When you're sat on the floor, changing your side-kick's nappy and she's wriggling like an eel and up to her neck in poop, you may wish you had more than two hands. Here's a tip - use your feet. No, don't change the nappy with your feet. What are you - a chimpanzee? Instead, put your legs either side of her and wiggle your feet to distract her. It will help stop her from moving about and making the mess worse than it already is. If things are really bad, you can even pin her down with a leg whilst you change her. She won't like it but needs must when you're trying to contain a poopastrophe.

Having retreated to the changing facilities, armed with my flowery Cath Kidston change bag, I quickly discovered the full extent of the damage. It was a river of evil smelling chunky mustard. It had leaked down her leg, up her back and as I stripped her off and reached for the wet wipes, I discovered there were only two left. Let us be frank, this was not a two wet wipe situation. Ideally, I required a team of trained professionals in heavy duty biohazard suits. But I didn't have those either.

I stripped my daughter and dangled her over the hand basin, creating a makeshift bidet. I won't lie. It wasn't a pretty scene. Brown water sprayed everywhere, on the taps, up the mirror. Utter carnage. There were no paper towels, so I improvised (badly) and wiped everything down best I could with my bare hands, before belatedly discovering the toilet paper and thinking 'Why, in God's name didn't I use this in the first place?'

On the subject of wreaking havoc on public toilets, as a man you will, at times, find yourself at a disadvantage. Most public places, that is shopping centres, museums, airports and the like have recognised that men, as well as women, change nappies and make sure the change facilities are in some neutral territory, like a disabled toilet.

Unfortunately, this won't always be the case. So, what do you do, if the only facilities are in the women's toilets? It's a strange sensation. Entering a women's toilet feels like entering forbidden territory. It reminded of the first time my dad took me through the darkened doors and frosted windows of a betting shop to have a flutter on the Grand National.

Alternatively, you could improvise and go al fresco. A pushchair, car boot or patch of floor in a quiet corner can suffice, but what if you really must use the change room in the ladies? It's a tricky one. I found knocking loudly on the door and asking permission from any occupants will usually provide a sympathetic response. 'Of course, my dear, we've all been there. I wish my husband had changed more nappies'. After all, you do have a good reason for being there. It's not like you're going in to snort cocaine off the toilet seat with a hooker on your lap, is it? Those days are well behind you now.

That said, my presence in the ladies has raised a few eyebrows as well as the occasional filthy look, so my advice is to tread carefully, be respectful and get the hell out of there as fast as your baby will allow.

Bananamour

D id you know, you share fifty per cent of your genetic make up with a banana? Ridiculous, isn't it? No, I don't believe it either. Yet, these unassuming fruit, bunched up in the fruit bowl between the apples and pears are pure yellow magic. It's going to be useful for you to understand the mysterious powers of the banana because it may mean the difference between your baby being a happy hippo or a miserable monkey. The difference between a peaceful night's sleep or hours of intermittent screaming and you gently banging your head against a wall in resigned desperation. Let me explain.

You are now responsible for the welfare of your child and a great part of their wellbeing, and yours, will be defined by how well they eat and what they eat. As your baby's diet moves from a milk dependency to solids, their gut will go through a great change. Their poop will change and how often they poop will change. Unpleasant, isn't it?

You will find that managing their diet will be a constant tightrope act. You don't want them to have an upset stomach, due to too much soft fruit and not enough starch, but you really don't want them to be constipated either. Did I say that the worst thing you will face is the awe inspiring mess of a public poonami? Sorry, but I lied. Take my word for it, there are few things as heart breaking as the tortured scream of your constipated child..

Squeaky was constipated, off and on, for several weeks. I gave her dried fruit, I gave her more fluids. I stopped giving her carbohydrates. I marinated her in oil and gave her tummy a rub (clockwise, not counter-clockwise). I went to the pharmacy and I went to the doctor. My lowest point in six months of non-stop parenting was the moment I had to poke a suppository up her bum. And if that wasn't bad enough, she kept on pooping it back at me, so I just sat there for two long minutes with my finger stuck where her sun doesn't shine, whilst she howled at me and I quietly swore to myself and tried my best not to cry.

And it still didn't bloody work.

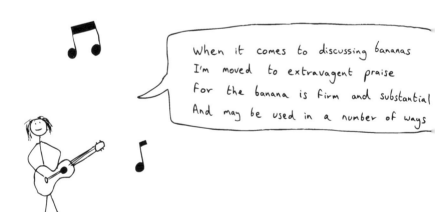

She was utterly miserable and would spontaneously burst into tears at any given time. She wasn't sleeping, so that meant we weren't sleeping. It was pretty desperate, until I gave her a banana at snack-time.

The thing is, you can't just use any banana. It must be the right type of banana.

The rule is - a soft ripe banana is terrific for debunging your baby if they're constipated. A firm banana is perfect if they have diarrhotea.

Remember that and you have solved the mysterious ways of the banana - the world will be your oyster (or your banana at least).

First words and other baby milestones

I s your baby on track, or are you an AWFUL PARENT who is FAILING your child? Sorry, I'm applying for a job with a popular tabloid newspaper and I got a bit carried away. Mums and dads are constantly measuring and comparing their child against the competition.

It's an easy trap to fall into. Everywhere, from nursery groups, health clinics to parenting books and now apps are providing a relentless pressure about the state of your child's development.

You probably shouldn't even read this chapter. Just flip to the next one. Oh, you're curious now? You still want to read it? Well, ok but it's really important you don't treat this chapter as a tool to measure your child's development and say "Oh no! I thought my baby was a genius but he's eight months old and hasn't achieved his diploma in advanced nose picking yet!" All babies progress at slightly different speeds and will hit these development stages when it suits them - so don't panic.

6 months

Your baby may be playing a new game called 'dropping things on the floor'. You might think she is doing this to deliberately aggravate you (she isn't yet, that comes later) but actually this is a big deal for her. She's learning about cause and effect. It's a basic version of Newtonian physics - if I let go of my toast (cause) it falls to the floor (effect). This simple action that we take for granted reinforces her understanding of how the world works. In my house, this looked rather like: grab broccoli, drop broccoli, broccoli falls, kersplat, daddy crawls about on his hands and knees with a wet wipe.

She's also more likely to take an interest in that timeless game of peek-a-boo, which is always a useful distraction technique for preventing your little one having a full-blown diva meltdown.

It's possible that your baby may start to imitate or mimic you. Don't build up your expectations too much though - she's not going to make you breakfast, but she might copy some of your hand movements, like wiping the food tray. Incidentally, you will still need to wipe down her food tray.

7 months

Your baby may start to crawl about now, or at least she is beginning to figure out how to coordinate her hands and feet. You can help her by leaving her on her tummy so she can wriggle her arms and legs in pitiful frustration. She will do a remarkable impression of a tired middle aged man (that's you) doing ten press ups e.g. lifting her chin off the floor and screaming.

Her little hands will have become more nimble too. Instead of clumsily grabbing things, she's learning how to work her thumb and forefinger to pick up and hold objects. When I say objects, what I mean is your face, so ears, nose and mouth. If you are particularly slow, she may go for your eyeball, so be vigilant and try to distract her with something less harmful like an AA battery or a tin opener (bloody hell, I was only joking, get that out of her hand right now!)

8 months

Your child is now thinking "Why am I the only one lying about on my back? Everyone else is standing, maybe I should try out this vertical thing". She's still too young to pull herself up so help her on to her feet and prop her up against the sofa. She's going to fall over, so pile some cushions around her to prevent a rude introduction to gravity.

Her memory is also developing. She will remember that if she pushes a ball, it rolls, or if she smacks her rattle against her toy box, it makes a noise. You should now expect your baby to hit everything she can, at every opportunity, with all the enthusiasm of a tiny Keith Moon or John Bonham.

9 months

Your child's first words will be one of the great steps in their development - that critical juncture when she begins to directly communicate with you. Will she say mama, will it be dada? The truth is it's kind of hard to say. Your baby will be babbling away and you will be listening intently to pick out sounds that appear to be words. To the best of my understanding, my daughter's first words were one of the following:

mu'umu'u - a loose dress of Hawaiian origin that hangs from the shoulder

mumu - nigerian slang used to describe a person who acts daft

moomoo - a new nightclub in Tunbridge Wells

I suspect Squeaky may be fluent in Finnish as well as Ewok.

Once, I was singing Prince's Purple Rain to her and she replied "En ymmärrä" (EN UUM-mar-ra) which is Finnish for "I don't understand". That struck me as remarkably perceptive. After all, when was the last time you saw a purple puddle? And she's often telling me "jub jub" which I'm sure is what the Ewoks say before they beat a stormtrooper to death with their tiny paws and use his head as a bongo drum.

Your child may also start learning to stand without your help. You'll probably discover this as she reaches for your mug of tea and attempts to knock it over your phone. Everything that you used to keep on a coffee table is now low hanging fruit, so you're going to have to put it all on the window sill. That includes coasters, drinks, remote controls, electronic devices, little pots of nick nacks, the contents of your rubbish bin - pretty much anything that isn't nailed down.

10 months

Your child is now learning independence. Do you remember how long it used to take to spoon feed a bowl of gloop into her? Well, now she's grabbing it from your hand and insisting she feeds herself. The mess will be utterly diabolical, but just remind yourself she's developing her fine motor skills as she successfully pokes spaghetti in her ear.

She also now understands that objects exist even when she can't see them. Life is now one giant game of Hide and Seek after another, with you concealing toys under cups or trying to hide the biscuits before she spots them and insisting on dried rice crackers instead of the mouth-watering selection of vegetables you set before her.

11 months

Your baby will be mobile around now, so good luck and don't forget the bubble wrap.

Their new-found independence may lead to them becoming more insecure. The theory goes that she's figured out that by doing things on her own, she's a separate person to you - and that frightens her.

Personally, I found the opposite to be true. Before she learned to crawl, Squeaky would freak out if she couldn't see me. As soon as she was on the move, she was much more confident if I was out of sight for a few moments.

It just goes to show that babies don't have a rule book and take enormous pleasure in defying your expectations. That said, you are unlikely to escape separation anxiety entirely. Babies always like to know there's someone nearby for a hug, or some attention, but be under no illusion, 'separation anxiety' is much more potent.

For weeks, I could barely lift a finger without Squeaky letting rip. To some extent I would let her cry it out, but when she got so upset she'd throw up over herself, then I'd pick her up and typically be unable to put her down again. I'd be holding her, whilst sorting the laundry, going to the toilet, cleaning my teeth – everything took five times as long, but on the plus side, my biceps toned up quite nicely.

12 months

Happy birthday! You might want to take a moment to reflect on your child's achievements in her first year. She's talking, but you're just not sure which one of the 6,500 known languages on the planet she's speaking. She's on the move, crawling and sofa surfing, maybe even walking independently. She constantly surprises you how much food she can put away, although - like me, you may be perplexed and disappointed to learn that your child has suddenly decided to refuse vegetables. I always thought it would happen later, when she sees her little friends refuse food, but no. One day your child is a sprout chomping machine, the next she's spitting them back at you like some Christmas themed cannon.

What would Darth Vader do?

If you are one of those guys who still wants to poke George Lucas in the face with a stick after his meddling with your childhood memories when he air dropped a host of CGI aberrations into the original Star Wars movies, then I have bad news for you, my friend. Even if the films hadn't changed, you have. As a father, I expected my world to be different. As a full-time, 24/7 daddy, I even found myself thinking about movies in a new light.

Here's a question - what do Marty McFly, Luke Skywalker and Indiana Jones have in common? The three greatest movie trilogies ever made? Ok, maybe, but what else? Let's just say none of their fathers are likely to own a 'Best Dad of the Year' mug.

On first appearances, Back to the Future appears to be a time travelling version of Chitty Chitty Bang Bang. It's about a kid with a skateboard and an ageing sidekick with hair like a toilet brush, isn't it? Well, on reflection the plot is really about Marty's dad, George and how he's utterly incapable of seducing the future mother of his own children. Ok. Marty mucked things up by travelling back in time and falling out of a tree, distracting his future mother with some weird oedipal flirting, but really? Didn't take much, did it? George is as wet as a flooded urinal on a rainy day in Margate, until his own son fixes everything with an unexpected guitar solo and a bolt of lightning.

It took the quest for the holy grail to reconcile Indiana (DON'T call me Junior!) Jones and his father. In The Last Crusade we learn that Henry Jones Snr was so singularly obsessed with his quest that Indy tells him "This is an obsession, Dad! I never understood it. Never! Neither did Mom!" Our hero's relationship with his father was so rotten he chose to be named after the family dog, rather than his own father.

And as for Skywalker, having your hand sliced off by your father during a ferocious lightsaber duel because you refuse to take his career advice is pretty harsh. Sorry Darth, but as much as you tried to reach out to your son, your career at the Death Star always came first - didn't it? You were second in command at the largest, most evil corporation in the known universe, eclipsing even Goldman Sachs. And to what end? The old dude in the dressing gown with the health and safety defective electrical hands was never going to let you be number one, was he?

I wonder sometimes how Star Wars might have panned out if Darth had been a more hands on dad from the beginning...

Location: Imperial Star Destroyer

> Darth Vader "I'd like to take some time out from crushing rebel scum to look after the twins, Luke and Leia, my master."

> Emperor "Lord Vader, I am disappointed in you. I have plans to build a powerful new weapon. I was expecting you to oversee its construction, but now I will have to ask Governor Moff Tarkin"

Darth Vader "I will teach the twins the ways of the force, my master."

Emperor "Very well. You can have six months on the usual Imperial maternity package."

Darth Vader "I wont disappoint you, my master."

Vader struggles to fit two child seats into his Tie Fighter and instead rents an old space freighter with plenty of luggage space for pushchairs, booster seats, change bags and all the other baby crap that he can't manage without.

After a few weeks of changing nappies, constant screaming and scraping baby puke off the ceiling, Vader takes the twins to the local Mos Eisley baby nursery. The mothers and infants of the local low life villainy and scum are scattered around the floor, singing 'Wind the bobbin up'. Every nursery, even those in a galaxy far, far away will sing 'Wind the bobbin up' despite having no idea what a bobbin is.

"How old are they?" asks a strange looking walrus creature.

"Seven months tomorrow" answers Vader. "They had their first food last week. Stewed bantha with prunes."

A few hum approvingly but one mum foolishly replies "Meredith had her first bantha when she was only five months old. But then she was always so advanced, (cough) ach, argh!"

Meredith's mother stumbles to the floor clutching her throat. Vader releases his grip and responds. "Luke is showing strong signs of the force. He levitated his first wookie this morning. Has Meredith levitated a wookie yet?"

Time passes and Vader takes the children to work for an unannounced visit to work. A storm trooper helps him with the buggy. "I would use the force" explains an embarrassed Vader. "But I haven't had a decent night's sleep in four months."

Not only is the Death Star a long way from being fully operational but it's quickly apparent there is a complete absence of changing facilities in the men's toilets. Vader marches over to the main control deck and insists the designers add a creche and baby feeding room. "But Lord Vader, if we add a creche there, the Death Star will be potentially vulnerable to attack from a single laser cannon shot from a low flying enemy craft. Why don't...(gurgling strangle noises)" Vader releases his grip. "Yes, Lord Vader, of course."

Superdad

All super heroes have a moment when they first discovery their extraordinary abilities. "Hey, Clark Kent, throw me the ball. Oh.." or "Peter Parker, nice to meet you. Eugh! You dirtbag! What the hell's that stuff coming out of your hands?"

I realised I'd developed lightning fast reflexes when my daughter was in mid-drop as she rolled off our bed. Beyond my wildest expectations, I spotted her, leaped across the room and caught her in one hand before she hit the floor. All in the blink of an eye. Not bad for a middle-aged man who has spent his entire life avoiding any kind of sporting activity.

As I spent more time with Squeaky, I noticed other super-human skills too, although they weren't as glamorous as lifting a bus with my bare hands:

1. I can smell a soiled nappy as soon as I enter a room. Ok, I'm never going to don a cape and save the world by knowing who has pooped themselves, but personally this was pretty remarkable. I can hardly smell anything due a twisted cartilage in my right nostril. Yet fatherhood mysteriously overcame this physical impairment and super-charged my nose

2. I can go from sound asleep to on my feet in less time than it takes to say "I feel a bit dizzy, can I go back to bed now?"

3. I get a strange tingle in my left ear when the house is quiet for too long. It invariably means Squeaky is eating the dirty tissues from the bin or she's smearing herself from head to foot in sudocrem

As well as heightened senses and quicker reactions, as a dad with a baby I found I was getting more attention from the opposite sex. One time, I was in the department store Liberty's, near Carnaby Street, pushing Squeaky about in the pushchair. My son was with my wife and her friend as they rummaged through the remains of the Christmas sale. I was briefly unchaperoned when an attractive young sales assistant approached me and asked if she could be of assistance.

"Oh, isn't your daughter a darling!" she told me. "You know, I never wanted children but now, I must say, you really have woken up my ovaries!"

Crikey!

"Is there anything else I can assist you with" she asked, with what might have been a glint in her eye.

What did I do, you might ask? Well, I mumbled my apologies and rapidly retreated as a good husband should.

You might be thinking - gosh, this would have been useful a few years ago when I was single. Well, here's a thought - do you have a friend who is unattached? Someone you can trust your baby with for a couple of hours? The best thing you can do is teach them how to change a nappy, lend them your baby and push them out the door. Women will throw the phone numbers at him, especially when they hear he's a kindly godfather giving a friend a break by taking care of their treasured love one. Thoughtful, selfless, responsible. Tick, tick, tick. Nobody needs to know your friend is ruthlessly exploiting your baby in the hope of practicing making babies. Anyway, it's just babysitting, right?

Dress code

Dressing your baby

I'll admit, for the first few weeks my efforts at dressing Squeaky were pretty cack handed. Her tights were often back to front and I made her wear a ghastly multi-coloured pointy hat that you only see on the heads of Glastonbury Festival goers. It really doesn't matter though - you can dress your child as a pirate or the Hungry Caterpillar everyday, if you like. So long as they're comfortable.

Just remember if she's wearing a hat or socks when you go out then there is a 95 per cent probability she'll remove them and drop them out the pushchair when she knows you're not looking. It's just a hat or a sock, you say? Well, yes but:

1. Her head and feet will get cold

2. People will assume I'm neglecting my child ('oooh, that useless father forgot her socks, poor thing')

3. Socks don't grow on trees

4. This is stage one of rebelling against her dad - if I don't stop the rot now, she'll be stealing cars and smoking crack with boys before I know it

I should mention that some clever shrew has invented the 'sock-on' which is a small elasticated strap that fits snugly over your child's socked foot. It's an ingenious invention that prevents your child wriggling out of their socks like they're a tiny Houdini, escaping from a set of handcuffs. The problem with sock-on's is that they're so tiny, they will disappear into your child's wardrobe and not be found again until she turns fifteen.

Dressing yourself

It's perhaps more important to consider what you should wear. You might be thinking, what possible difference does it make what I wear? True, it might seem more obvious that a mum who is breast feeding needs to wear something with easy access, but provides a degree of modesty. We dads don't have that particular problem, but I would like to make a couple of sartorial suggestions which may make your life considerably easier.

The first rule is sure, you can wear whatever you like, so long as you don't mind it developing the permanent aroma of rancid yaks yoghurt. I don't care what those Persil adverts say - there's something about milky baby vomit that is as durable as the stars, time and dried pasta. Push all your best clothes to the back of the wardrobe - it's time for tatting about in old jeans, worn out jumpers and t-shirts you really ought to have demoted to wiping condensation off windows.

Do not wear trousers with a buttoned fly. This is especially important if you are out and about. I found myself in the unfortunate situation of needing a wee and having to take Squeaky with me to the urinal. I'm holding my daughter firmly and securely with my right arm. I'm not going to drop her, but I'm down to one hand. Have you tried undoing buttons with one hand? It's tricky, but do-able. Doing them up again? That's quite a different matter.

There I was, hopping up and down with my daughter in one arm, trying to do my flies up. The floor was unpleasantly wet. One wrong footing and I was liable to Torville and Dean across the toilet floor and land face first in the urinal. It was a close run thing but fortunately I'd been to a roller disco once when I was thirteen so I just imagined they were playing New Order's Blue Monday and glided like a pro to the toilet door without my trousers falling down.

Do not wear shoes with laces. What do you mean, all your shoes have laces? Well, go out and buy some slip-ons or loafers. I hate to break this to you, but you no longer have the luxury of sitting down and using both hands to put on your shoes. Leaving the house will almost always coincide with your child having a hysterical outburst. Either she was tired anyway and you're taking her out for a nap in her pushchair or she thinks you're abandoning her and kicks off.

One afternoon, I was at my friend Emma's house and trying to leave whilst holding Squeaky who was experiencing a moment of incandescent rage. I was pathetically shoving my feet in my shoes without success, when my friend got down on the floor and tied my shoelaces for me. It must have been more than thirty years since someone else had tied my laces for me and I was quite overwhelmed with gratitude. But it was quite clear, to me at least, that I was utterly pathetic and needed a better plan.

There is a technique for doing up your shoe laces whilst balancing a small infant on your knee, which I am happy to share with you, but I warn you, it is tricky. To do up your right shoe, position your child on your lap, on your right leg. Then bend your right knee, resting your right foot on your left knee. You should now be able to put both arms around your child, to prevent her falling, whilst leaving both hands free to do up your laces. Did I mention this position incorporates at least three yogic positions? I call it the 'Warrior doing up his shoelaces'. Side effects can include a hernia, slipped disc and a dislocated knee.

Are you really still wondering if you need to invest in a new pair of slip on shoes?

Finding time for yourself

W hen you're with your baby 24/7 it's easy to get obsessive about your little one. Why does she still have that cough? Why won't she eat more? Why isn't she crawling yet? Before you know it, you're looking up tropical diseases on the internet and experiencing 'crazy parent disorder'.

To prevent your slippery slide down this rabbit hole of creeping madness, I suggest you find some time for yourself. I know it's not easy, I know your baby gobbles up your every living, breathing moment, but it's important, for your sake and theirs, to maintain some sense of balance in your life.

Keep up with your mates as best you can. Every two or three of weeks I'd go for a beer and a curry with a couple of friends. I enjoyed the rogan josh well enough, but the real pleasure was in simply walking out the house with no responsibilities and having a conversation about something other than my baby's bowel movements. It's very easy not to bother, especially when you're exhausted, but you'll be glad you made the effort once you're out, even if you are knackered and would rather be lying face down in a sensory deprivation tank.

When Amy was on maternity leave first time around, we signed her on to an evening class every Tuesday. She'd return home with elaborate orchids she'd made from sugar paste and wire. No, you couldn't eat them. Not without needing dental work afterwards. Yes, she could have used the extra sleep but getting out the house to do something creative definitely helped recharge her batteries.

I learned to play the piano. I know, on reflection it seems bloody unlikely doesn't it?

My uncle Charles offered me a lovely upright piano, black with corinthian columns. I figured the kids would learn when they were a bit older. Then, I thought, stuff that, what about me? Then, a friend recommended a local piano teacher, Cathy, who happened to be on leave with her baby too.

What would you like to learn, she asked. "I'd like to play the blues like an old New Orleans dude in the 1950s" I explained during our first lesson, rather hopefully.

Of course, even aging boogie-woogie masters have to start with the basics. And so, my piano practice progressed slowly with "C, E, G <Waaaaargh!!!> G, E, C <Blood-curdling scream!>" Squeaky would sit in the highchair next to me, as I relentlessly bribed her with raisins and rice crackers.

Am I any good? You know those prodigiously talented small children who can belt out Rachmaninov before they're six years old? Well, I'm the opposite of that, being neither young (kissed forty goodbye) nor especially talented. Can you imagine the sound a piano makes when you drop it down a flight of stairs? Well, I'm a little more tuneful than that. Still, I'm not doing too bad considering Squeaky's frequent heckling. After all, I doubt Elton John practiced the keys whilst a small monkey threw raisins at him.

Are you baby sitting today?

I t's not that unusual to see a dad out and about with a baby in a pushchair, but it's usually under the assumption that you're 'baby sitting' for an hour or two. On any number of occasions, I found myself politely explaining that actually I had been 'baby sitting' my daughter for several months. It's a simple enough assumption and I don't think any harm was ever meant by it. There are times though when society's inability to quickly recognise the role of a dad can create a problem.

Take parking the car. There I am, carefully reversing into a 'parent-and-child' parking space so that I can open my door and retrieve my daughter without dinging the car next to me. I look out my rear-view mirror and a woman is slowly cruising past, muttering pointedly and scowling at me. It's pretty clear she believes I've swiped some mum's parking space. A moment passes before she realises her mistake and that I actually have a baby in the car, before she accelerates away.

These sort of challenges are even more of a problem if you don't have your baby with you. What do I mean? Let me give you an example. I'm on the London Underground with a pushchair and a baby (my baby obviously) and opposite me, a mother is wrestling with her small infant who is demanding cake/biscuits/a small pony but what they really need is a mild sedative. I don't mean to but I catch the mum's eye and wordlessly, exchange a sympathetic glance. She recognises and returns the gesture in a brief moment of solidarity from a fellow parent and returns her attention to her offspring.

Now, let's repeat the situation, except I don't have a baby or a pushchair. I'm on the London Underground, returning from work. Opposite me, a mum is trying to rationalise with her increasingly fraught toddler who is demanding the moon on a stick. I didn't mean to catch the mother's eye but I do so and again, attempt to convey a sympathetic smile. This time, she looks at me like I'm dog shit and I half expect her to point at me and shout "LOOK OUT! THIS MAN IS A PAEDO!"

I can't help thinking the situation would have panned out differently if I'd been a fellow mum. Perhaps we might not have laughed, gone for a coffee and connected on Facebook, but her reaction might have been rather less hostile.

This wasn't a one-off instance. It happened a few times (although not always so severe) before I realised I had lost my full-time dad credentials if I didn't have the kids. The danger was that I had got so used to strangers being more friendly and open when I had Squeaky with me that I was woefully ill prepared for this sudden and dramatic change in my status when I left the house unaccompanied. It was as if I'd lost my back stage pass, had my ID checked by security and been promptly thrown out of the nearest window.

This sort of casual undermining happens to dads a lot. A colleague told me how her father was helping out at his grandson's school sports day. A child fell over in front of him, clearly hurt and upset. The grandfather stepped forward to check he was ok but before he could do so, a mum (not this boy's mum, just someone elses mum) said "Let me, you don't want anyone getting the wrong idea". Now, I suppose she meant well but she clearly implied that this man, or any man, had no business stepping up and checking on a hurt child. The grandad now feels that he can't get involved, for fear of what people might think.

I tried to find other dads who had looked after their kids full-time to find out how common these attitudes were. With no small amount of irony, I found a few dads on Mumsnet in an obscure blog called 'Fatherhood'. Most of them had positive experiences of fatherhood and looking after their child, but nearly all of them had shared similar negative experiences:

"I used to ask school about coming on day trips / helping out. Nada. Was told they were over subscribed etc. Then one day got an invite, and wouldn't you know it, it was all men / dads. They must have planned it out. That was the one trip of the year dads got a look in."

"I've grown used to being patronised by the occasional woman. Often older women rather than mums of young kids. I've still yet to work out how to respond when someone suggests what I'm doing is brave."

"Most women who I've spoken too at parks or at kids play centres at weekend's think I'm a dad who's split up from my partner and having my son at weekend's . When I explain that I'm a full time single dad just about everyone give me praise and think I'm amazing taking on a so called "a mum's job"

"I don't know if it is because I live in a quite middleclass area but every pram club or library reading group i went to treated me like a fart in a lift."

It does rather feel like a role reversal of what women went through in the 1960s. "Oooh, a lady in the office - you're a feisty one. Cambridge degree, you say? I'll have my tea with milk, two sugars and be quick about it, sweet cheeks"

Come on mums - and dads, for that matter, it's the twenty-first century for flips sake.

A brief history of dads

Are dads more hands on than they used to be? I think so. I was born in 1975. My dad never changed a nappy, but then I doubt many (or any) of my mates dads did either. Roles were pretty clear. Fathers only ever touched a vacuum cleaner if it needed fixing and mums dealt with the babies. As I got a little older, if I was misbehaving, mum – as a last resort - would threaten to "Tell your father" and that would be enough to rein me in. That was about the extent of it. Things changed of course and as I got older my dad taught me to swim, play pool and chess, drive a car and showed me how to snap a man's leg like a dry twig.

It got me wondering – have dads always been like this? I don't know, perhaps Lord Admiral Nelson potty trained his kids? Maybe Stone Age dad took his baby along to hunt woolly mammoths? Who knows? So, I had a little poke about and to be honest, the history of fatherhood was full of surprises.

Pre-historic dad

So, dad left the cave armed with his club to hunt animals?
Mum stayed home with the babies to stitch animal hides and
cook tasty, but soon to be extinct, animals over a roasting
fire? Well, apparently not. At least, not often. Apparently,
in most tribes, dad was around the home most if not all the
time. Usually, both mum and dad would hunt and forage
nearby and dads would be very hands on with bringing up
the kids. In particular they would often carry their infant
children, to keep them safe from predators and open fires.

It has been suggested that the early development and success
of the human species may be at least partly due to ancient
dads helping out at home. Anthropologist, Lee T. Gettler,
suggests the population of our ancestor Homo genus grew
larger and more quickly than its ape competitors because
dads shared the child rearing. A helpful dad gave mothers

the opportunity to recover from childbirth more quickly and have more children and larger families. A man who could demonstrate his ability and willingness to help carry, bathe, feed, play and teach children was more appealing to females. Bluntly, pre-historic dad realised pretty quickly he was more likely to get more sex if he was a better dad. And no, before you get any ideas, I don't think that's still true today.

Peasant dad

Many of us have a vague understanding that unless our ancestor had the exceptional good fortune to be born into aristocracy, where they drank, plotted marriages and flogged peasants to pass the time, then more likely they were just peasants. That meant, men ploughed the fields whilst the womenfolk helped one another with the cooking and looked after the babies. There's some truth in that, but it really depends where in the world you are.

In Northern Europe dads had always been very active parents. They needed to be. Life expectancy wasn't great so grandparents often died before their grandchildren were born. People migrated a lot around the country, so you couldn't always depend on a neighbour to help out. And women usually had a job themselves, such as weaving. Perhaps more surprising, there's evidence that dads cared for children and did the housework to leave the women free to work. Take a look at this lullaby:

Hush thee, my baby
Lie still with thy daddy,
Thy mammy has gone to the mill

To grind thee some wheat

To make thee some meat (confusingly, this meant bread)

Oh my dear babby lie still

If you worked the fields, your working day was dictated by the available daylight, so in winter dads spent much off their day with the family at home.

And it wasn't just the peasants. Historically, lone parents were men, not women. In the event of divorce, custody of children often went to fathers and some eight per cent of mothers died in childbirth. It's estimated that between 1599-1811, about one in four children lived with their fathers and not their mothers, compared to only one per cent today.

Industrial revolution dad

The industrial revolution was a game changer in terms of parenting and rather stuffed things up for dads. As work shifted to the factories, fathers increasingly worked away from home. Women took over 'traditional' fathers' tasks – such as educating children and dads became increasingly absent from the daily upbringing of their children.

Dads gained a bad reputation and Victorian fathers in particular are regarded as aloof and distant disciniplarians. This may be yet another myth about fatherhood. Dr Julie-Marie Strange (superb name) is a social historian at Manchester University. She scoured hundreds of contemporary sources – from memoirs to music hall comedy lyrics – to see what fathers in the 19th and early 20th Century were really like.

What she discovered was that working class dads were far more affectionate and involved than we give them credit.

The vast majority talked about fathers who were fun, who spent time with their kids in their spare time, dads who taught their children to be interested in the world and how things worked. Funnily enough, a common theme in Victorian comedy showed a father left in charge of the children while the mother goes out - only for everything to descend into utter chaos. It sounds remarkably like an episode of The Simpsons and just goes to show how little things have changed.

Returning to work

The day will come when it's time to hang up your Cath Kidston change bag, remove the emergency sudocream, odd socks and dirty wet wipes from your pocket and try to remember how to have a conversation about something other than poop. Maybe you're relieved about returning to work or maybe you're not, but one thing is for sure, it will come around much faster than you expected.

Brace yourself for the first time you drop your little one off at nursery because it is a real killer. Squeaky howled at me as I passed her over to her key worker. I have no shame in admitting I wiped a tear from my eye as I closed the door behind me. I felt terrible, as if I was abandoning and neglecting my daughter. After a week or so though, it became pretty clear her little cry would last all of thirty seconds before she was distracted by a piece of toast. How do I feel about being so easily replaced by a small piece of crispy bread? Pretty good, really. I can go to work happy in the knowledge that Squeaky is squeaking with happiness.

The next stage may be even trickier though. This may come as something of a surprise, but going back to work is likely to be quite a culture shock. Mums have known this for years, but for dads It's something of a new experience and there are a number of stages you're likely to go through:

1. I'm free! Oh, the pleasures in simple things. You can get a coffee without wondering how you're going to drink it whilst managing a pushchair with one hand. You can go to the toilet whenever you want. You can have real, grown up conversations about anything from Bake Off to behavioural psychology. You don't have any wet wipes - and it does not matter! No one is crying. No one is screaming and no one has shit themself (probably).

2. Missing limb syndrome. After the intoxicating euphoria of freedom comes the abiding thought 'Argh! I've lost my child!' I'd compare it to the sensation people sometimes feel when they have had some terrible accident and lost a limb. They know their left arm is no longer there but on some level their body doesn't believe it and wants to have a good scratch.

You have become so habituated in having them at your side, day and night for so long that part of your brain is sure you should still be looking after them. Do not panic

- once these different parts of your brain have had a short conversation with one another your heart rate can return to it's normal non-life threatening levels. Try to avoid having this chat with yourself out loud and in a public place though, or your colleagues will assume you have lost your marbles.

3. Guilt. It's finally sunk in. You are sat at your desk dealing with idiot emails and your child is in the arms of, let's be honest, some stranger who is enjoying the experience of watching your child grow up. You feel like you have abandoned them. I know I did. Sure, your child's nursery has professional, caring staff and you know she's in safe hands and enjoying herself, but it's not the same, is it? The guilt will subside but it might never entirely leave you. You just have to find the right work/life balance that works for you and delicately weigh the need to earn a living and have a satisfying professional life against the needs of your child and your need to share time with them.

4. Sitting on your arse. It depends on what you do for a living. I spend eight hours a day sat in front of a PC screen. I suppose I have always done this and forgotten there could be an alternative. When I looked after Squeaky, I was always on my feet, mixing milk bottles, disposing of nappies, washing up, picking her up or pushing her about in the pushchair. Suddenly changing from running about all day to sitting down all the time was restful at first. Soon enough, I'd look for spurious reasons to get out of my chair. I knew I had a problem when I found myself at a dispensing machine buying a Kit Kat. I didn't really want one. I just wanted to go for a walk.

5. Brain mush. Mums call it baby brain. You spend so long with your child that your brain becomes reprogrammed to remember all the verses of The Wheels on the Bus, but you can't concentrate on reading a Word document for longer than twenty seconds. It took me a few weeks to get my head around spreadsheets and feel like I wasn't horribly out of my depth. Don't write yourself off, give yourself some time to get back into the swing of things and if all else fails, do what I have always done - bluff your way through work.

6. You may be surprised to learn that you have picked up some useful skills that transfer from running around after a baby to holding down a job in an office. Being a parent is the most demanding job of all. It requires patience, endurance, efficiency, understanding and laser precision time mannagement skills. Negotiating with tricky colleagues or demanding clients will be a walk in the park after mastering the tantrums of your child through day and night. Just remember that you can't use the naughty step at work, however much you think they deserve it.

Is it worth the trouble?

I hope you haven't read this book and come to the conclusion, sod that for a game of soldiers - I'd rather sit at my desk, have meetings and spend time with people who won't throw up over me. Yes, a stay at home dad spends a considerable chunk of his time up to his elbows in water to a soundtrack of incessant screaming. Yes, you'll wonder if you have accidentally been booked into Guantanamo Bay, to spend your days being bombarded with 'white noise' torture by a furious and tiny Donald Rumsfeld. Yes, you will be tempted to 'lose your shit' several times a day. Yes, you will forget what a normal conversation sounds like. And yes, it's quite likely your employer might be under the delusion you have taken several months holiday and your career might suffer, but...

It is worth it. It really is. Every damnable, frustrating, poo soaked, screaming moment of absolute frustration.

As a father taking care of a baby full-time, you are leading the greatest social revolution since women were liberated by the pill in the 1960s. Incidentally, the bra burning is something of a myth so put your pants back on - no one wants to see you burn your britches. But seriously, this is historic stuff. Women will only have equality at the workplace when men have equal opportunities to bring up their children.

By taking on parental responsibilities full-time, you are changing the future and if you have a daughter, you are subtly improving her employment opportunities. After all, how can an employer discriminate against a woman if her male partner might be the one taking time off work to bring up the baby?

Does it make you a better father? Well, that is a matter of opinion, but you will be a more experienced parent. According to Malcom Gladwell, it takes 10,000 hours practice before you can excel at something. The Beatles clocked up their hours playing back-to-back gigs in Hamburg, Tiger Woods, Bill Gates and Andy Murray - they all had to put the hours in, before they became the best. There's no reason to assume parenting isn't the same.

To put this into perspective, one month of full-time childcare will chalk you up 730 hours. So, what does putting in these hours actually mean? Well, I noticed I was

much better at reading my daughter's signals. I can now distinguish between 'Waah!' (I'm hungry) from 'Wargh!' (I want a cuddle), as well as 'WARGH!' (I'm tired) and 'Waah!' (my gums hurt). All this took hours and hours of trial and error. Mums call it 'womens intuition' - it's not though, not really. It's just hours and hours of experience. I'm no expert though. After six months intensive hands-on experience, I'm not even half-way to the big 10K with only 4380 hours, but I look at it this way, at least I can cope if my wife is late back from work.

This investment of your time buys you a bond with your child. It is inevitable that you will become closer. Having spent all this time in your company, she will feel closer to you and feel more comfortable and confident around you. Six months is just a fraction of your life to date, but it's half her entire life. You are her world - you feed her, entertain her, keep her clean and safe. She may never remember the particulars as she grows up, but the bond you have developed will always be there and you will be around to remind her that you will aways be there for her, when she needs you.

I would suggest being a full-time dad might make you a better husband too. I developed a great deal more understanding and respect for my wife and what she does. Instead of assuming it's not an easy gig, I can safely say that I know it's not easy. I'm never going to come home and wonder why the laundry hasn't been folded and put away, because I know how demanding a small child can be. I'm never going to look at a group of mums in Starbucks, laughing with their babies and think 'that looks easier than working' because I know they are probably laughing hysterically as they swap stories of being awoken repeatedly and spending their days being thrown up over.

And don't forget those super-powers you'll develop, such as cat like reflexes, eyes in the back of your head and the ability to sniff out an errant poo from one hundred feet. You will also develop the ability to do most things whilst holding your baby with one arm - make breakfast (seriously, this is impressive, try buttering toast with one hand), eat a meal with one hand, do the laundry, tidy the house, go to the toilet (a great deal of care is required).

I'm not saying that being proficient in cooking a meal with one hand is a transferable skill that will impress your employer. But your time-management skills will be sharper than a butchers blade. Your ability to multi-task and juggle tasks will be unsurpassed and you will be adept at managing difficult situations.

Still not sure? Let me put it this way. You love your family, right? Of course, you do. But do you remember what it was like when you first fell in love? That sense of giddy intoxication and infatuation, a little bit of obsession, that hunger to be near and close to someone? I felt that everyday I spent with my daughter.

Instead of noticing changes in her development once every week or two, I had the time to spot all the little incidental changes, each and every day - the first time she noticed her toes, the first time she smiled at her reflection in the mirror, her first attempts to crawl.

Being a parent might be bloody exhausting, but it's also relentlessly satisfying because you can take credit for her growing and developing into the funny, smart and beautiful little person that she is becoming. You did that. Sure, the hours are terrible, there's no sick leave and the pay is worse than minimum wage - but it's still the best job in the world.

Acknowledgements

This book would never have been possible without the love and support of my wife, Amy.

I'm indebted to Nick Gammons, Mark Storey, Mary O'Meara, Jay Neale, Amy Kwok and Barbara Tindale for reading early drafts of 'Daddy Day Care' and giving me their support, thoughts and suggestions.

Thank you to Gavin Dupee for typesetting the book and designing the cover, without whom this book would be still stuck on my Samsung tablet.

Thank you to Fanoosh, Catherine and everyone at Growing Tree nursery for taking care of my daughter so I could return to work in the knowledge she was in a safe, loving environment.

The song lyric quoted in the banana chapter is 'Banana Hymn' by Kevin Ayers.

HYMN
BY KEVIN AYERS
(C) BLACKHILL MUSIC LTD (PRS)
ALL RIGHTS ADMINISTERED BY WARNER/CHAPPELL MUSIC LTD
ALL RIGHTS RESERVED

And thanks to the Fatherhood Institute for providing much of the information in 'A brief history of dads'. They're a terrific organisation, lobbying government on behalf of fathers and collating all sorts of fascinating dad related research in the UK and internationally. Do look them up.

About the Author

Jonathan Tindale is five foot, eleven and a half inches tall and has a thing for hats. He lives in suburban London with his wife, Amy and two children. He loves tea, burns toast and tries not to swear when he treads on the lego. When he's not running about after the kids or at work, he's learning to play the piano. He'd like to play some Dr John or Jerry Lee Lewis but is still on page three of 'Boogie Woogie for Beginners'.

He started writing when he kept a journal whilst falling over mountains in Nepal. Some years later he persuaded his employer to pack him off to live in a caravan in New Zealand. It took him the best part of a decade but this experience became his first book, Squashed Possums.

Jon's plan to circumnavigate the globe in a milk float were swiftly abandoned with the arrival of his children, so he thought he'd write about being a dad instead, which he realised is a far greater adventure.

Please consider writing a couple of words about the book on Amazon or Goodreads.

Or you can contact the author at jontindale.com and Twitter at @jontindale.

Squashed Possums

2016 Award Finalist - Travel Non-Fiction - Readers' Favorite Awards

Ten years after returning from the New Zealand outback, Jon receives a mysterious manuscript in the post. Narrated by Jon's former home, the lone caravan, Squashed Possums reveals what it's like to live in the wild through four seasons, including New Zealand's coldest winter in decades.

Discover how Jon finds himself reversing off the edge of a cliff, meet the Maori chef who survived 9/11, the pioneers who paved the way, and catch sight of the elusive kiwi bird. Encounter hedgehogs that fly, possums that scream, and perhaps most importantly, the lone caravan with a story to tell...

Bill Bryson, best-selling author of Notes from a Small Island "Terrific"

Giles Milton, author of Nathaniel's Nutmeg "The caravan narrator – yes, a first. May it sell in the millions"

Dr Jock Phillips, NZ historian and author "I thoroughly enjoyed it! What an interesting story"

Available now in paperback and kindle

Squashed Possums

Introduction

L et me be honest with you, I do not know who wrote this book. A few weeks ago, a package arrived at my home. A brown jiffy bag. There was no return address. No explanation as to who, or what, had sent this to me. Inside, was a thick wad of loosely typed papers. The pages were a little worse for wear, and worn around the edges with a faint whiff of the country. As I sat down to read, I was even more shocked by the words that jumped out of the wrangled pages.

More than a decade ago, I had lived in a caravan in New Zealand. It was what the locals referred to as a lone caravan, a ramshackle place in the middle of nowhere, so far removed from suburban life that it had no address. This was the wop-wops, only to be found by traversing a long and winding dirt track, rutted with hazards and holes. For several months, I had made this strange place my home. I grew to both love and, at times, hate this place. But I cannot deny the extraordinary effect it had upon me, and upon the contents of this mysterious book.

The package reveals an account of my life in this place. From the moment I reversed off the edge of a cliff and almost tumbled into the oblivion, to my close encounter with a possum, it's all there. The long nights enveloped in darkness, with nothing but the stars for company and how, for a moment, the experience turned my head inside out.

On the subject of mind altering experiences, not only has someone else written my story, but they've also used extracts from my diary. How the author came by it, I cannot say, but another narrator is involved and this voice is definitely not mine. And who is it that shares their account of such a strange tale? None other than the caravan itself.

God damn! What madness is this, you ask. Yes, you heard me right. The narrator of this book is none other than the caravan. Or so it appears. I cannot comment on the provenance of the author. After all, I received this book anonymously. But before you get wrapped up in wondering how a vehicle could perform such a feat, let me tell you that this is a vehicle with a story to tell.

This lone caravan it is one of the last of its kind. It is iconic in its own quiet, unassuming way. There are books and photographic galleries dedicated to it. To the casual observer, it is an eyesore, a large heap of junk waiting to be swept away and replaced by something cleaner and more comfortable. Yet this place is a prominent pointer to the country's past, a time when pioneers lived on the fringe of civilisation and endured the elements without any modern conveniences. Brave and resourceful souls found ingenious ways to construct what they needed from scraps of wire and metal, lessons that have been learnt and passed on to this very day.

This is the story of one such solitary caravan; a tale about life in a wild, untamed place in contrast to the rest of the modern world. New Zealand has always been a remote place, with strange and unique wildlife that has evolved through the protection of thousands of miles of sea from the nearest predator. New Zealand was the last significant land in the world to be colonised by people. Polynesian explorers arrived some eight hundred years ago and many centuries later, the Europeans made their discovery. The collision of these two peoples continues to reverberate to this day, as the country deftly balances accusations and reconciliation thanks to the Treaty of Waitangi.

More than a century and a half after the Treaty, New Zealand has grown to a modest population of 4 million. You don't have to travel far to lose yourself in an isolated place. The country's cities and towns are dwarfed by the vast swathes of forest and wilderness. So, perhaps this book is not so strange after all; for who better to tell the tale of remote New Zealand than the lone caravan itself.

Not just a caravan

I'll bet you ten bucks you've never read a travel book like this before. A travel book written by a caravan? A lone van out in the wild? I wasn't always an inanimate object. I know a thing or two about travelling. I have been hitched to the back of many a vehicle and pulled all the way from the Pacific Isles of Northland, down to the bleak township of Invercargill in the south. But no longer. We all have to retire someplace and here I am, a simple wagon perched on a small scenic hill far from the nearest town, in a place sometimes romantically and a little cryptically referred to as the 'wop wops'.

Hang on, have I misled you already? I am not just a caravan. Let me offer you my dimensions. I am two caravans, one smaller, one larger, connected by a short umbilical corridor. As you can imagine I am not as mobile as I once was. My wheels have long since been removed and replaced with short stumps of tree trunk. I'll admit, at first it was embarrassing. Whoever heard of a caravan without wheels? But I learned to live with the ignominy. What choice did I have? At least I don't have to worry about getting a puncture and falling over.

Above me stands a slanted corrugated metal roof that valiantly attempts to protect me from the elements. It's not a thing of beauty it must be said, but it keeps me dry. The rain bounces off it with a rat-a-tat-tat like the trigger happy gunfire in a Rambo movie. My roof is held in place by several wooden beams that plunge vertically and diagonally all around me. You might say they embrace me and hold me together.

Of my two caravans, the smaller one contains a simple kitchen, furnished with a pantry of spices and a temperamental fridge. There's no oven. Instead there's a camping stove with two electric hobs, and a microwave that might pre-date the Apollo missions. A small laminated formica table has seen better days, and is beginning to peel around the edges. Outside, sat on my tow cable sits a loud, clumsy washing machine that shakes and clatters whenever it's used. Trust me, it's an earthquake trapped in a white metal box.

My second van is a larger model, with panoramic windows from the bedroom through to the library. Whoever is staying with me can hardly complain about the view. There is an epic vista of forested hills and the grass is startlingly green. At night, the light of the Milky Way pours through my windows, our spiral galaxy as effective as a thousand 100 watt bulbs.

A small iron stove stands next to the double bed. Slapped on the chimney is a yellow post-it note that reads: 'Do not use!' The rusting chimney was blocked some time ago, and has not since been fixed. The useless stove is a constant reminder to any tenant that when winter approaches, my central heating is not so much inadequate as non-existent.

I did mention a library, but I'm no stately home, so don't get any far fetched ideas. There's little room to spare, but an entire wall is chocka with shelves and these shelves are stuffed with books. The contents make for an eclectic literary time capsule. A weathered volume of Brecht and Chomsky paperbacks stand beside the well-thumbed poems of Hafiz. The great Sufi master sits next to the collected works of Shakespeare. I absorb information when I can, reading over the shoulder of whoever is staying with me at the time. The radio is a pleasant distraction, but I have no such luxuries as a television, hot running water, internet or even a bathroom.

I do have a bath though. A bath in a caravan? Well, sort of. Let me explain. On the edge of a nearby stream, or ditch rather, stands a typical household ceramic white tub that's currently half full of dead leaves and green stains. If you're so inclined you can fill the bath from a hot water hose, or with a bucket of ominously green and cold stream water. The stream mostly consists of slimy algae, which isn't an appealing prospect I must say. I wouldn't be too impressed if someone tried to wash me with frog flavoured ditchwater...

Those of you paying attention may have noticed that I didn't mention a toilet. Well, I don't have one. But my tenant doesn't have to make like a bear and bury his business in the woods each day. Instead, there's a small building with a gas powered shower and hot water about five minutes walk away. Each call of nature requires a head long scramble down an almost vertical slope, only to meet the pine forest and trudge through the thick, pine needle strewn undergrowth. You have to traverse the hill like a, what do you call them, oh I remember, a slalom skier, a few steps left and a few steps right, cautiously sliding your way down. And yes, I have seen more than a few visitors slip and fall face first into a tree.

You have the measure of me, but I ought to introduce you to my latest resident. Jon is a young bloke, still in his twenties and standing a frustrating half inch below six feet tall. I'll tell you now for nothing that he's bound to bump his head on my door frame a few times, before he remembers to duck. He seems to have temporarily replaced Anne, who lived with me these past few years and then mysteriously packed her bags and left last week. We'd been together long enough that she'd learned to adapt and adjust to living here in the wild woods, but Jon looks more than a little lost. He's got a lot to learn, to really understand what it takes to live in the wop-wops.

This story isn't just the tale of a lonely van, but of this young man's life here. I don't try to imagine what is going through his head. I am not a psychic caravan. I leave that to the Romany caravans and their shiny crystal balls. Jon keeps a journal and every night he scribbles away in his erratic scrawl. I am not ashamed to admit that I intrude on his privacy and read over his shoulder from time to time. After all, there's no telly so what else is a van to do for entertainment? I don't think he'd mind if I shared the occasional diary entry with you. After all, this is his story too.

Saturday 1 March

What had I done? What is this place? I'm not sure if my jaw dropped, but my stomach certainly lurched sideways as I faced these strange surroundings. I actually felt nauseous. The truth of what I'd done finally dawned on me. When I'd planned to come here it seemed like an adventure, moving to this peculiar and distant caravan in the hills of New Zealand. I'd seen photos on email from the comfort of my own home in London, but nothing could quite prepare me for how rustic it was. No, not rustic, but primitive. Like a pioneer's wood cabin, far removed from society, a place of almost absolute solitude. How on earth they'd ever managed to move the vans up this hill was a complete mystery. Looking around, I realised that I'm surrounded by forests, and not even the slightest sign of human life. I had no idea where the middle of nowhere was, but it looks like I'd not only found it, but I'd made it my home.

Getting to my new home was no simple task. On first arriving, I'd been collected from the nearest town, Paraparaumu, by my neighbour Jean. She collected me in a beaten up white Mazda and we quickly left town, crossing the train tracks and heading for the hills. The Maungakotukutuku road is a zig zag route with hairpin bends that cling to the side of the vertigo inducing valley. To our left a steep hill rose above us. To our right, a sheer vertical drop revealed itself with the road plunging into the distant forests below. Climbing up the valley, the road reached level ground and the tarmac soon turned into gravel. The Mazda bounced along the dusty unsealed track, giving off clouds of dust as it flew across the uneven slippery surface. My first feeling was absolute shock, followed by a dash of wonder and a great deal of near terror. Where on earth were we going? I'm clumsy by nature and I was none too confident about driving to my new home every day without calamity.

What bright idea had brought me here

exactly? Well, I'd exchanged my one bed flat in suburban west London for a caravan in the New Zealand bush. I'd also swapped working for the government with working as a librarian in the small town of Paraparaumu. Living in a van might sound a bit desperate, but I'd decidedly rejected a comfortable life in favour of my solitary home in the woods. Other exchange offers had included a woman who had contacted me from Hamilton, further north towards Auckland. She'd offered me the use of her comfortable suburban four bedroom house, and was even willing to throw in her husband as part of the package. She figured that her other half could keep me company while she's away, which struck me as odd to say the least. Unsurprisingly, a spell in surburbia complete with a househusband was not the slightest bit appealing. Other opportunities came in from the Australian outback, Canadian British Colombia - where the nearest neighbour appeared to be a bear, and a sunny spot near Bondi Beach in Sydney. I turned them all down in favour of living in the bush. Madness? Perhaps. But as soon as the photos of the rag tag lone caravan appeared in my inbox, I was hooked.

Reflecting on my primitive new home, I tried to remind myself why I was doing this. My intention at first had been simple enough. Escape. Working as a civil servant in London, I recall the feeling of restlessness in my job. I'd started to feel like a cog in the machine, staring into a PC screen all day long, tired of reminding myself that this was better than working in an asbestos factory or gutting fish for a living.

One month before I left London and chaos was all around. It was February 2003. London was preparing for a terrorist attack and the impending war with Iraq had left everyone nervous. The newspapers were filled with threats of poison gas being pumped into the London Underground or even a rocket attack over Heathrow. There was a palpable tension in the air. Only two weeks before my departure, I had returned home from work, shoes caked in snow, after another painfully slow journey battling through London's paralysed tube, train and road network. Kicking my shoes off, I'd put on the kettle, sat down, switched on the television and watched a documentary simulating a radioactive dirty bomb at Trafalgar Square, promptly devastating central London, not a hundred yards from my office. Perhaps moving twelve thousand miles to a remote caravan in the woods wasn't such a bad idea after all?

But if I'm honest, there was always more to this than escape. After all, I hadn't met many people who'd willingly swap the comforts of their own home for what was essentially a hut in the woods. I'd always felt a connection to wild places, and as a child I had whiled away many a carefree hour swinging across rivers on rope swings. I have fond memories of my father building a shelter in the woods, using nothing but branches and vines. It was great fun enacting the Arthur Ransome and Enid Blyton stories that my mother had read to me, and far more exciting than the troubles of school. But playing in a forest for an hour or two before returning to my home comforts and loving family was quite a contrast to moving to a forest, some twelve thousand miles away.

End of diary entry

.

Printed in Great Britain
by Amazon